Basic Skills Reading Comprehensi

Table of Contents

Frank Schaffer Publications®

Instructional Fair is an imprint of Frank Schaffer Publications.

Author: Cindy Karwowski
Project Director/Editor: Sharon Kirkwood
Editors: Elizabeth Flikkema, Kathleen Vaughn
Cover Artist: Cindy Cutler
Interior Artist: Barb Lorseyedi
Production: Pat Geasler

Send all inquiries to:
Frank Schaffer Publications
8720 Orion Place
Columbus, Ohio 43240-2111

Name _____

Circus Stars

The circus is coming to town. Everyone loves the circus! The Stromboli Brothers' Amazing Animal Circus is very special. Animals perform astonishing tricks never before thought possible. Often the animals are more clever than human circus performers!

Follow the directions.

1. Draw a 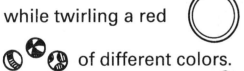 hanging by its tail from the trapeze while peeling a with its feet.

2. In the center draw a gray balancing on one back while twirling a red around its waist. Also, have him juggle three of different colors.

3. Draw and color a brown in the left ring holding a . Show him taming two yellow .

4. In the remaining draw three in clown suits. Use five different colors to decorate their costumes. Add some props.

5. Draw the in front of the center ring.

Circus Stars

Use with page 2.

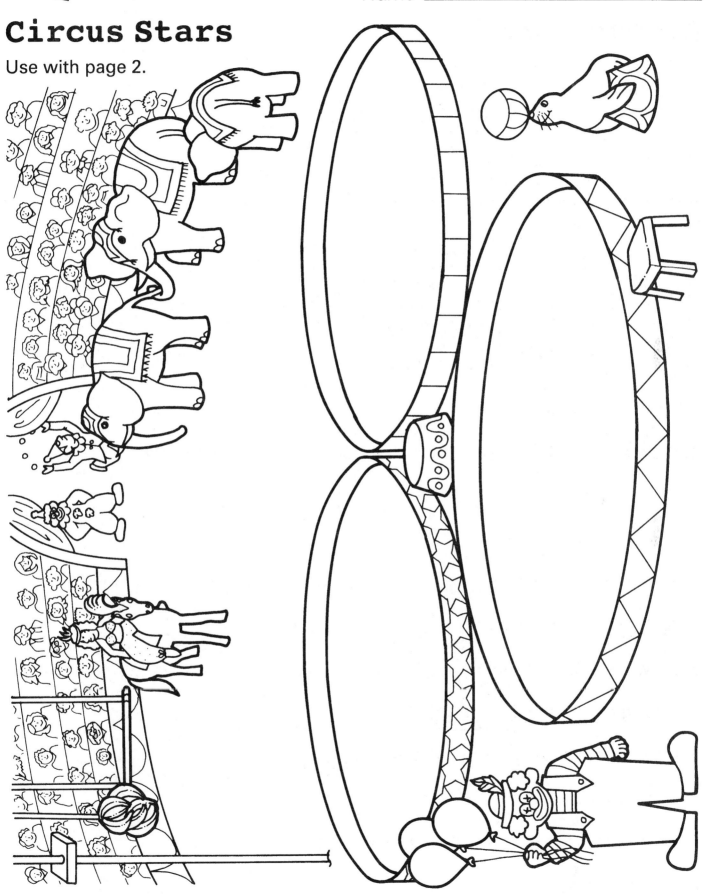

Name _____

A High Fly

Hee and Haw are announcing the last half of the final inning of the World Series.

"The Toledo Toads are really bugged now!" said Hee.

"Last year the Houston Hornets really stung them, and the Toads are looking to get back at them this year," replied Haw.

"If the Toads can stop the next batter, they'll be this year's winners!" remarked Hee.

"Uh, oh! It's a high fly ball! Wart, in left field, is frantically hopping backwards. Can he get there in time?" shouted Haw.

"Amazing! Wart just stuck out his long tongue, and caught the ball! The Toledo Toads win!" yelled Hee.

"Yes, time's fun when you're having flies!" cheered both announcers.

Write the correct number order under the baseballs to tell the main idea.

Hornets   Houston   Toledo   The   Toads   beat   the

____   ____   ____   ____   ____

Circle five words in the Wordsearch that relate to toads and hornets.

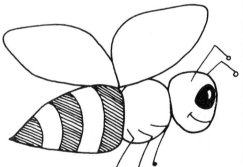

C	K	F	L	I	E	S
G	E	L	W	A	R	T
F	S	L	S	J	K	U
B	U	G	G	E	D	N
H	O	P	P	I	N	G

Circle the correct answer.

The characters in the story are probably

people

animals

because _____

Name _____

Plop Goes the Weasel!

"I'm so sick of that weasel sneaking up behind us!" complained Bitty Mouse.

"It's time we taught him a lesson!" decided Buster.

The two mice thought of a plan. They went to the store and bought a whistle and a slingshot.

The next day as Sneaky Weasel came near their hole, Buster jumped off a fence and landed on the weasel's tail. As the weasel opened his mouth to scream, Bitty pulled back on the slingshot and launched the whistle down the weasel's throat.

"At least now we'll hear him coming because he will 'weasel' while he works!" giggled the mice.

Cut out the pictures at the bottom of the page and glue them in correct order on the cartoon strip below.

1	2	3	4	5

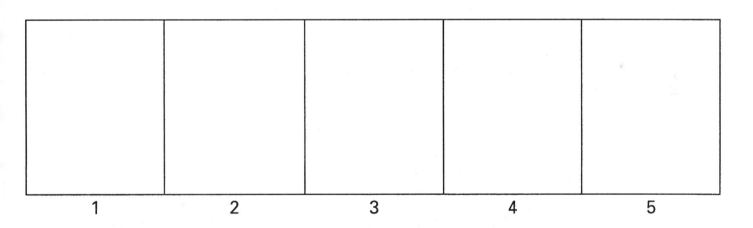

Name _____

The Cat's Meow

Sometimes Leo acts so strange! Two weeks ago he thought he was a duck. All day long he walked around wearing flippers on his feet and flapping his arms. When asked what he wanted for lunch, he answered, "Quack-ers, quack-ers." Last week he claimed to be a lightning bug. He even tied a light bulb on his back. When I asked him why he didn't light up, he said that his batteries must be run down. Well, today he thinks he's a cat. He has been purring since breakfast which, of course, was a bowl of milk. I warned him to stop jumping off the back of the couch. He says he doesn't need to worry because he has nine lives. Hmmm . . . I wonder how he'll like his dinner tonight? I have a little rubber mouse, and . . .

Unscramble the letters to write the name of the correct animal.

1. If Leo walks around shaking a rattle, he probably thinks he's a

_____ .
        (kaltsnetrae)

2. If Leo paints black and white stripes all over himself, he probably thinks he's a

_____ .
        (arebz)

3. If Leo gobbles his food and sticks feathers in his clothes, he probably thinks

he's a _____ .
              (etrkyu)

4. If Leo wears a sweatshirt with one large front pocket and hops around, he

probably thinks he's a _____ .
                            (gaoknroa)

Extension: What might Leo do if he thought he were . . .

    a dog? _____

    a bunny? _____

Name _____

Bunches of Love

Chester Chimpanzee had a crush on Chelsea, the cutest monkey in the jungle. He wanted to send her a special valentine. Chester scratched his head, wiggled his ears, and wrinkled his nose as he thought very hard. Finally, he ate a banana and sent Chelsea the peel. Chelsea looked puzzled until she read the note that came with it.

Roses are red;
Bananas are yellow.
You "a-peel" to me;
I'm your secret fellow!

Color the banana that tells the main idea, yellow. Color the other bananas green.

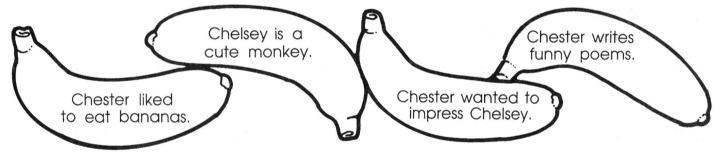

Chester liked to eat bananas.

Chelsey is a cute monkey.

Chester wanted to impress Chelsey.

Chester writes funny poems.

Which animals might send these valentines?

Roses are red;
Peanuts are tan.
I love your long nose
And your ears like a fan!

Roses are red;
Tree leaves are green.
Your very long neck
Is a reaching machine!

_____   _____

Extension: Pretend that you are an animal and write a valentine poem to a friend.

Name _____

A Lot of Hot Air

Patrick bought fifteen sticks of bubble gum for the price of ten. He began putting the gum into his mouth. One, two, three pieces fit easily. Chomp! Chomp! Four, five, six were next. Chew! Chew! Seven, eight, nine, and so on, until all fifteen pieces filled his mouth. After a few small practice bubbles, Patrick decided that he would try to blow the biggest bubble ever. Slowly, he filled the bubble with air. It grew and grew until he tipped his head back and blew one huge puff of air.

Just then, something happened! Patrick felt his feet slowly lift off the ground. He looked from side to side and noticed he was staring at the tops of trees. He looked down and saw the top of his house.

A few moments later a tiny bluebird landed on top of the bubble. As the bird pecked at the bubble, its beak poked a hole in the bubble, and whoosh! Patrick began floating down to the ground. Luckily, he landed on top of a haystack. As he slid down, he thought to himself, "Next time, maybe fourteen pieces would be safer!"

Circle the correct word to complete each sentence.

Patrick chewed   ten / fifteen   pieces of bubble gum.

A huge   bubble / wind   lifted Patrick off the ground.

Patrick saw the tops of   trees and his house. / mountains.

A   haystack / bird   popped Patrick's bubble.

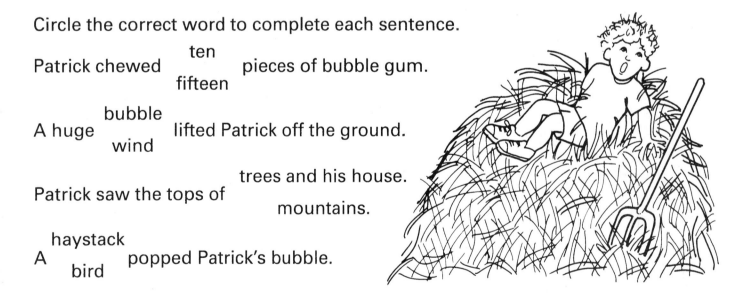

Extension: Pretend you are above looking down. Draw the top of . . .

a boat.   a snowman.   an elephant.

Name _____

Magic Wishes

Four animals found a magic lamp. They rubbed the lamp, and a genie appeared.

"I will grant each of you one wish," announced the genie.

"Make my trunk smaller!" demanded the vain elephant. "I wish to be the most beautiful elephant that ever lived."

"Make my legs longer!" commanded the alligator. "I want to be taller than all of my alligator friends."

"Make my neck shorter!" ordered the giraffe. "I am tired of always staring at the tops of trees."

"Dear Genie, please make me be satisfied with whooooo I am,"

whispered the wise, old owl.

Poof! Kazaam! Their wishes were granted. However, soon after, only one of these animals was happy. Can you guess whooooo?

Write the letter on the line that shows which activity each animal could no longer do.

____ The elephant could no longer   a. eat leaves from the tops of trees.

____ The alligator could no longer   b. spray water on itself.

____ The giraffe could no longer   c. swim unnoticed in the water.

Why was the owl so wise? _____

Write about something that you wanted, and what happened after you received it.

_____

_____

_____

Extension: Draw a picture of each of the animals after it had gotten its wish.

Going for a Ride

Name _____

Welcome to the Amazing Adventure Theme Park! This park has many exciting new rides.

Use the Word Bank to write the name of each ride that fits in the boxes below. All names will be written across →.

Word Bank

Aladdin's Lamp	Magic Carpet	Comet Crash
Sea Kingdom	Crater Dip	Glass Slipper
Meteor Bumper	Monster Mash	Tilt-a-Whirlpool
Ride-the-Waves	Make-a-Splash	Flying Saucers
	Big Dipper	

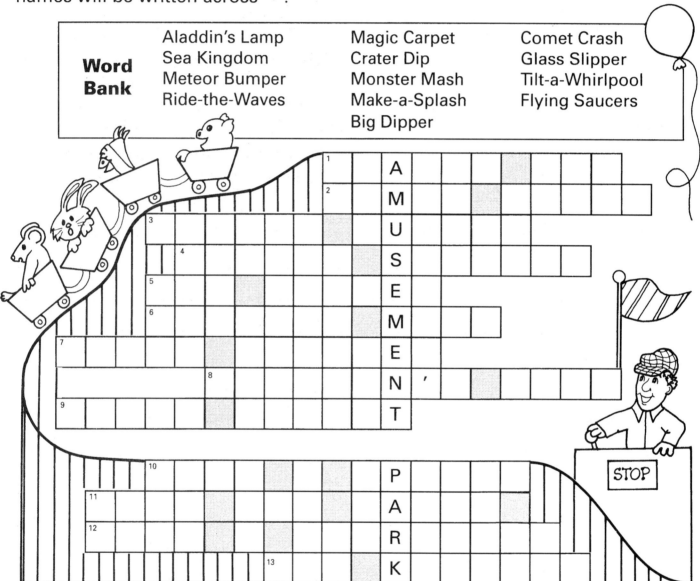

The theme park has three areas: Fantasy World   Water World   Space World

Tell which areas in the park the rides belong.

Rides #1 – 5 belong in _____ World.

Rides #6 – 9 belong in _____ World.

Rides #10 – 13 belong in _____ World.

Name _____

Itsy, Bitsy Spider

One sunny afternoon Stan and Ollie were chasing each other around the yard. After a while, they both grew tired and decided to rest in the grass. As they rested, the boys noticed a tiny spider begin to climb into a drain spout.

"You know about the itsy, bitsy spider don't you?" asked Ollie. "Let's see what will happen."

"I'll get the hose and squirt water into the top of the gutter. You watch from the bottom and see if the spider comes down," suggested Stan.

So, Stan turned on the hose and aimed it at the top of the gutter . . .

Tell what you think happened next. _____

_____

_____

_____

Draw an escape plan for the spider. Include all of the characters from the story. Label the parts.

Name _____

Digging for Treasure

Petey and I decided to dig for buried treasure. I wasn't sure where to start, but Petey had a feeling that we should dig behind the big oak tree. So that is what we did.

We dug for hours. Our pile of dirt was growing taller by the minute. Suddenly my shovel hit something hard. Petey and I became excited, and our hearts began thumping. We dug faster and faster. Soon, we had uncovered what seemed to be a gigantic bone! Maybe it had belonged to a dinosaur! I imagined bringing it to a museum and receiving an award. I turned to tell Petey about my thoughts, but when I looked around, he and the bone were gone!

I searched for hours. Eventually, Petey came home, but without the bone. Had he re-buried it in his own secret place, or had he chewed on it until nothing was left? Petey isn't really much of a scientist!

Circle the correct pictures.

How many shovels were used in the story?

 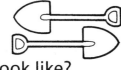 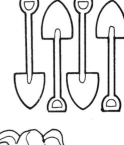

What does Petey look like?

Underline the correct phrase.

1. The girl became excited because she   thought she had found a dinosaur bone.

                                       found lots of money.

2. Petey became excited because he   liked to study about bones.

                                       had found a delicious dinner.

Digging for Treasure

Use with page 12.

Use the Word Bank and the riddles to write what kind of bones Petey and his friend discovered on later "digs."

Word Bank

lamb	cow
chicken	mouse
porcupine	squirrel

Don't give me oil when I squeak.

_____

You can't pull the wool over my eyes after I have a haircut.

I crossed the road once too often.

_____

I grow my own set of toothpicks.

"The Nutcracker" is my favorite ballet.

_____

_____

My favorite movie is "The Sound of Moosic."

_____

Name _____

The Perfect Excuse

"I don't see your homework," announced Mrs. Crabtree.

"Don't you see my paper?" I answered. "I put it on your desk."

"All I see is a blank sheet of paper," she said.

"Wow! Then it must have really happened! Last night when I sat down to do my homework, I thought I saw two giggling ghosts fly into my bedroom. They offered me 'ghoul-aid,' and I drank a full cup. All of a sudden my toes and legs disappeared! Before I could yell out, my whole body had become invisible!"

"Oh, really!" said Mrs. Crabtree, looking confused.

"However, Mrs. Crabtree, I knew I had homework to finish, so I kept on writing after they left."

"And then what happened?" asked Mrs. Crabtree.

"When I woke up this morning, I was happy to see that I was no longer invisible! My homework is proof that this really happened! Those silly ghosts must have given me invisible ink to write with!"

Write the good habits in the heart and the bad habits in the ghost.

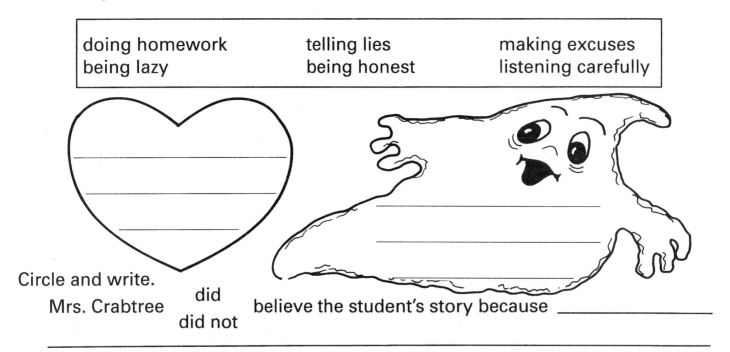

| doing homework | telling lies | making excuses |
| being lazy | being honest | listening carefully |

Circle and write.

Mrs. Crabtree   did
                 did not   believe the student's story because _____

Name _____

What's Up, Doc?

"Open wide!" ordered Dr. Allswell. "I want to check your tonsils."

The patient did exactly as he was told. The doctor sprayed the animal's throat with medication. "Your sore throat should feel better by tomorrow," said the doctor.

The next patient hobbled into the office.

"I can see that your knees are swollen. I'll wrap them and give you medicine to help get rid of the pain, but please try to lose a little weight. Carrying too many extra pounds can make your legs cramp and feel sore."

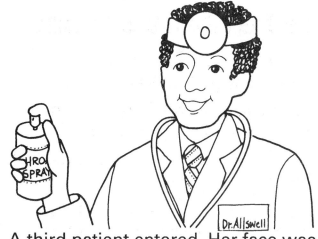

A third patient entered. Her face was very puffy.

"Well, I notice that you have been stung by several bees. My nurse will give you some medicine to help the swelling go down. Try to stay away from those little critters."

On the line next to each animal, write the letter that shows what it's problem was.

____ The elephant   a. had lots of bee stings.

____ The bear   b. had a sore throat.

____ The giraffe   c. had swollen knees.

Use the Word Bank and the clues to complete the puzzle.

Word Bank	alligator	monkey	kitten	centipede	seal	snake

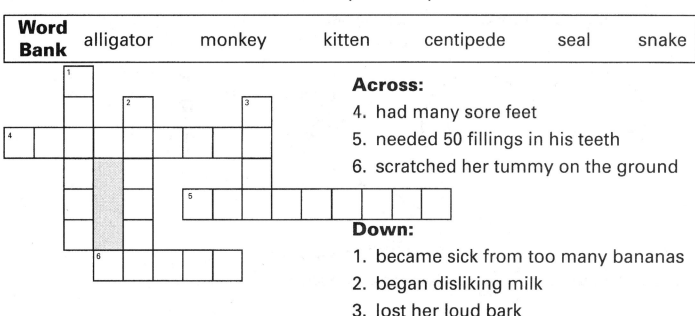

Across:

4. had many sore feet

5. needed 50 fillings in his teeth

6. scratched her tummy on the ground

Down:

1. became sick from too many bananas

2. began disliking milk

3. lost her loud bark

Name _____

A Hare–Raising Experience

Jack Rabbit loved to grow carrots. First, he found a diamond-shaped field. Next, he carefully planted and watered the seeds. Then, he watched as the little green tops of carrots began pushing through the dirt. Finally, 83 carrots were ready to be pulled from the earth. Jack indeed had the only 83-"carrot" diamond in town, and he proudly gave it to his friend Jill.

Number the sentences in the correct order.

____ The carrots were ready to be pulled.

____ Green carrot tops started popping up from the ground.

____ Jack watered the carrot seeds.

____ Jack found a field.

____ Jack planted carrot seeds.

Jack was always busy. Fill in the blanks with letters to show what he did.

```
        P           L
        U       F ___ U N D
        L           V
    G   L           E
  W ___ T ___ R  E ___
        V   D
        E
```

Laugh a Little: Write the scrambled letters correctly on the line.

After Jack and Jill got married, they went on their _____ moon.
                                                    (ynnbu)

Name _____

Seeing with the Heart

Tina was in a silly mood. She thought it would be fun to close her eyes when deciding what to wear for Grandma and Grandpa's visit. So, with her eyes closed, she pulled out a heavy red and blue sweater from the bottom drawer. From the next drawer she grabbed a pair of purple polka-dotted summer shorts. She laughed out loud when she saw that she had chosen one orange knee sock and one yellow-striped ankle sock from the top drawer. From her closet, Tina grabbed one summer sandal and one cowboy boot. She then added a pair of silly sunglasses and a huge baseball cap.

The doorbell rang. Grandma and Grandpa walked into the house. "You are even prettier than I remember," said Grandma sweetly.

"You'll always be our little grandbaby, no matter how grown-up you become," said Grandpa proudly.

Tina wondered why they didn't laugh or ask why she was dressed so silly. Do they need new glasses? No, she knew Mom was right. Grandparents' love is just very special!

Check the correct answer in each sentence.

Tina decided to play a trick on her grandparents because . . .

☐ she was in a silly mood.
☐ they liked to surprise each other.

Tina's clothes didn't match because . . .

☐ she was colorblind.
☐ her eyes were closed.

Tina's grandparents didn't care how Tina dressed because . . .

☐ they were colorblind.
☐ they loved her however she dressed.

Extension: Draw and color Tina's clothing as described in the story.

Mother Knows Best

Before she left for the store, Mother told her two children to stay in the yard. But, Ding and A-Ling did not listen. Instead, they jumped into their little spaceship and flew off to another planet. After landing, they left their ship and began to explore.

They walked through parks, visited factories, talked to traffic lights, raced with airplanes, and lost track of time.

When they finally looked at the time, they rushed to their planet, hoping to get home before their mother returned from shopping. But they were too late!

"Where on Earth have you been?" asked Mother.

"Wow, Mother sure is smart!" they thought.

Ding looked at A-Ling. "How did Mother know?" he gasped.

Follow the directions to see how Ding and A-Ling looked.

1. Connect the dots to form each head.
2. Draw three square eyes and a large oval nose on each face.
3. Give each face a large, happy smile with 8 pointed teeth on Ding's face and 6 rectangular teeth on A-Ling's face.
4. Give Ding 4 large ears and A-Ling, 4 small ears.
5. Draw two wavy antennae on the top of each head.
6. Color each face using 6 colors.

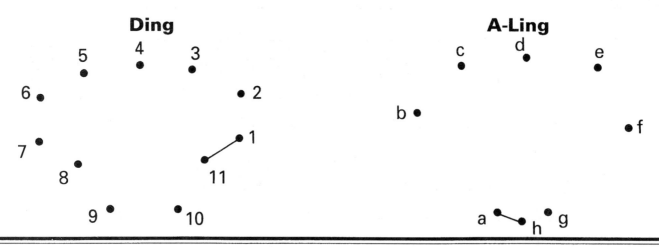

Name _____

Word Power

On a warm day last summer, my brother Bill gazed at my father, yawned and said, "I'm bored!"

"Really?" said Father. "Come with me." So Father took Bill outside.

"I bet you won't be bored while you wash and wax the car!" Father chuckled.

Bill scrubbed, rubbed, dried, and waxed for three hours. When he was finished, he was so tired he took a nap for the rest of the afternoon.

Another time Dad wanted to play golf. So he found Mom and began, "Honey, I'm bored . . ." Before he could finish telling Mom about his golf

plans, she had him mowing the lawn and cleaning the garage.

Even my four-year-old sister, Margo, isn't safe. One day when she was a little cranky, she let those two little words slip from her mouth. Before she could wrinkle her nose and pout, Mom had her picking up all of the toys scattered on her bedroom floor!

Well, I'm too smart to ever say, "I'm bored!"

"Am I glad you said that!" said Mom. "Come here . . ."

Tell what you think happened next.

_____

_____

Tell what happened to each person when he/she said, "I'm bored!"

Bill had to _____

Dad had to _____

Margo had to _____

Underline the correct phrase.

Mom and Dad gave jobs to the family members when they were bored . . .

    because the family members are lazy.

    because Mom and Dad don't want others to have fun.

    because there was work to be done.

Name _____

Distant Relatives

Yesterday my friend Rex and I visited the museum. We were excited about seeing the new dinosaur display.

"Wow!" I yelled when I looked up at the skeleton of the tyrannosaurus.

He's my distant cousin," said Rex proudly. "In fact, I was named after him!"

"My cousin was really a picky eater," giggled Rex. "He's no skin, just bones!"

That night while sleeping, I dreamed of that tyrannosaurus. I imagined him sticking his head into my bedroom window. I was too frightened to scream. When he opened his huge mouth, I froze.

"Do you know what happened to me because I wouldn't take a bath?" thundered the dinosaur.

I shook my head.

"I became x-stinked!" he roared.

I have now decided that both Rex and his dinosaur "cousin" must be related. They both tell bad jokes!

Both Rex and his "cousin" liked telling jokes. Circle the five words that best describe them. Then write the words in the boxes.

Hint: Write the longest word first.

sad	crabby	comical
silly	loud	mad
scared	jolly	brave
funny	quiet	pranksters

Name _____

Hide-and-Seek

The jungle animals were playing hide-and-seek. Gorilla thundered, "I will be 'It'!" The other animals ran away quickly.

Leopard hid in the middle of a field of giant polka-dotted flowers. Zebra ran behind the tall, dark reeds in the water. Poor silly Elephant didn't know what to do.

"Where can I hide?" he wondered. "I must look carefully."

Finally, Elephant caught up to Mouse and stood behind her.

"I'll hide behind you because we are the same color!" he cheerfully explained. Mouse agreed.

Write the names of the animals on the lines.

Two animals that hid well are _____ and _____ .

Two animals that are not very clever are _____ and _____ .

The only animal in the story who can walk on two legs is _____ .

The two animals most different in size are _____ and _____ .

Write two ways in which all five animals are alike.

_____

_____

Extension: Where might the following animals hide? Be creative.

peacock _____

skunk _____

_____

_____

snake _____

alligator _____

_____

_____

Name _____

Going Fishing

It was a lazy, summer day. I was fishing down at the river.

Suddenly a strong tug jerked me to my feet. I struggled to reel in a large colorful fish who said, "Greetings."

My mouth dropped and my eyes grew wide. The fish said, "Come, meet some of my friends. We'll show you how to really play 'Fish'." He yanked me into the water, gathered his strange fish friends and got a deck of cards. We played "Fish" for several hours. It was fun! He said that maybe tomorrow we could play "Eel of Fortune."

That evening, Dad asked me what I had done all afternoon.

"Oh, I just went fishing," I answered.

Unscramble and write the missing words. Then follow each direction to complete the picture on the next page.

1. The large, yellow _____ fish had huge red _____
   (kaltnig)   (spli)
   and wore funny _____ on his face. (Draw and color him near
                        (ssglase)
   the rock.)

2. I met a little _____ fish who wore an orange _____
   (lube)   (bsaeblla)
   cap. (Draw and color her near the tall plants.)

3. A pair of green and purple _____ fish had curly, red _____ .
   (ristped)   (hria)
   (Draw and color them inside the tire.)

4. An old, yellow-and-brown polka-dotted fish used his long _____
                                                        (onse)
   to deal the cards. (Draw and color him with the cards near the treasure chest.)

5. A pink _____ was swimming toward the reeds. (Draw and
          (mslona)
   color him swimming in the correct direction.)

Name _____

Going Fishing

Use with page 22.

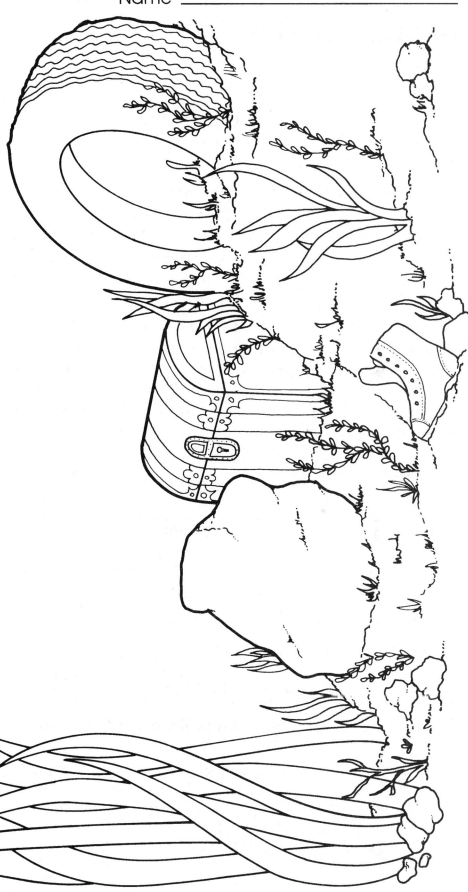

Baseball Fever

Bobby's favorite sport is baseball. He tries to play every day. Snow, ice, and rain don't stop him from practicing; he just hits crumpled paper balls in the basement.

Bobby even dreams about baseball. If one dream ends before the game is over, he continues the same dream the next night just so he won't lose his turn at bat! And when Bobby isn't dreaming about a big game, he's counting baseballs flying over the stadium while he's dozing.

Sometimes Bobby even daydreams about baseball while he's talking to someone. When his dentist asked him which tooth hurt, he answered, "First row, left field."

Bobby plans to become a major league player. "I can see my picture on a baseball card some day. Children will ask me for my autograph. Maybe I'll even have a candy bar named after me."

Write the missing details from the story on the blank lines.

1. Bobby hits _____ in the basement when he can't practice outside.

2. Bobby begins new dreams where old ones leave off so that he doesn't

   _____.

3. While he is dozing, Bobby counts _____.

4. One day Bobby hopes to write his name on a _____.

5. Bobby would like to have a _____ named after him.

Extension: Draw your picture on the card to show what you hope to be doing some day. Be sure to autograph the card.

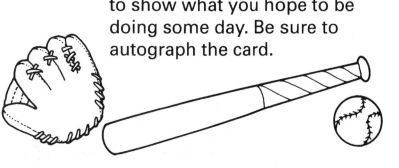

Name _____

A Helpful Hint

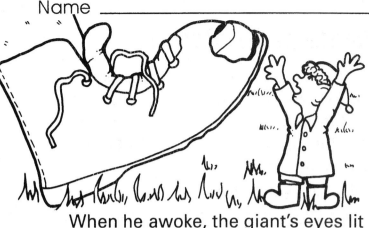

One day a very poor and ragged giant was walking in the forest, when he heard a tiny voice say, "Look out! You are going to step on me!"

The giant bent down and looked carefully around him. "Sorry, little guy," said the giant. "I didn't see you standing there. You should wear a bright red outfit so that I can see you better."

"That's a good idea," replied the elf. He thanked the giant and ran off to join his family. The giant didn't see his friend for a long time.

The Christmas season had always been a sad and lonely time for the giant. On Christmas Eve he turned out the lights in his broken-down house and went to sleep.

When he awoke, the giant's eyes lit up. He saw that his house had been painted. New clothes were hanging in his closet. A pile of gifts sat in the living room. He did not understand what had happened. Then he bent over and looked closely at a red spot on the rug.

The elf explained, "Santa hired our family to help deliver presents. He liked our red suits. If it weren't for your suggestion, we would never have gotten these jobs. Thanks, big guy!"

Circle the correct character in each sentence.

1. A poor and ragged   giant / elf   was walking in the forest.

2. The   giant / elf   was almost crushed by a big foot.

3. The   giant / elf   had an idea.

4. The   giant / elf   had no family.

5. The   giant / elf   was hired by Santa.

6. The   giant / elf   returned a favor.

Name _____

What a Mouthful!

Clark wanted to make a super sandwich. He gathered food from the cupboards and refrigerator. First, he sliced a long loaf of French bread. Then he spread some butter on the bottom slice of bread. After that, he carefully added sweet pickles. On top of that he added cold meat. Next, came some cheese. Then Clark placed the tomatoes and, finally, the lettuce.

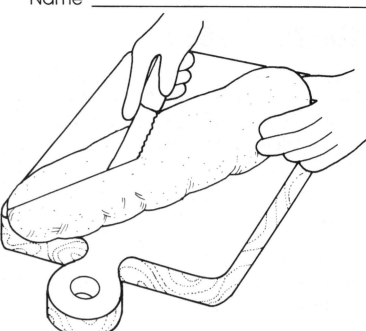

Make Clark's super sandwich. Use the sample pictures as models for your drawing. Draw and color the food in the correct order between the French bread slices.

| cheese | tomatoes | cold meat | lettuce | sweet pickles |

The Blizzard

When Crystal went to bed, it was just beginning to snow. "Maybe there won't be any school tomorrow!" she hoped. Then she fell asleep and began to dream . . .

When she opened her eyes, Crystal looked out the window and only saw white! "Our house is completely buried in snow!" she thought. "We won't have school today, or tomorrow, or maybe even all winter!"

"Wait a second!" she thought. "Now I won't be able to see my friends. I can't visit Grandma and Grandpa. Who knows when I will go to the store or the movies, or anywhere again!" Crystal was worried but fell back to sleep.

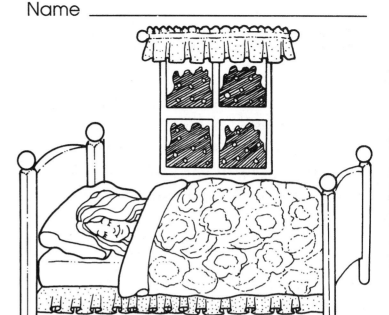

Then Crystal felt her mom lightly shake her. "Crystal, it's time to get up and go to school."

Crystal raced to the window. There was only an inch of snow on the ground. "I'll be ready in a few minutes," she said as she began to grin.

Use the Word Bank to write how Crystal feels in each sentence.

Word Bank	happy	excited	worried	hopeful

1. Crystal sees the snow begin to fall and thinks that maybe there won't be

   school tomorrow. She feels _____ .

2. When she sees the heavy snowfall, Crystal realizes that school will be closed.

   She feels _____ .

3. Then Crystal realizes she won't see friends and grandparents if she can't

   leave the house. She feels _____ .

4. When Crystal gets out of bed she realizes she was dreaming. Crystal feels

   _____ .

Extension: Write how you feel when you discover school will be closed for the day.

Name _____

Grandma's Birthday

Grandma Tortoise was having another birthday. Her friends decided to throw a party for her and give funny presents because Grandma loved to laugh.

Grandma finally arrived at the party—late as usual! "I had to stop at the Shell Station," she giggled.

Then the hare announced, "I planned a race for your party, but then I remembered that you always win. So, I'll save time and give you the trophy now!"

Grandma got lots of presents, but she had two favorites. The first was a green army helmet. Grandma chuckled when she took it from the box. "It reminds me of my first boyfriend. He had the best-looking shell in town," she remarked.

The other present that Grandma liked was a sweater with tiny yarn people sewn all around the neck. Grandma had lots of turtleneck sweaters, but this was her only "people-neck" sweater.

At last, it was time for the cake and ice cream. There was only one problem. The ice cream had melted by the time Grandma had blown out all of the candles! Everyone agreed that at Grandma's next birthday party they would eat the ice cream first!

Circle the correct detail in each sentence.

Grandma Tortoise was   early / late   for her birthday party.

The hare thought Grandma   would / would not   win the race.

The army helmet reminded her of an old   boyfriend / hat

Little yarn   turtles / people   were sewn on the neck of the sweater.

Circle Yes or No for each sentence.

Grandma liked . . .		Yes	No
	to be on time.	Yes	No
	to laugh.	Yes	No
	funny presents.	Yes	No
	her sweater.	Yes	No

Name _____

Look Out Below!

"Help! There's a really big monster under Charlie's bed!" screamed Amy, as she peeked below my bed and ran out of my room.

"You're right!" said Kevin. "He is mean and ugly, and I know that he'll eat Charlie as soon as he gets into bed!" Kevin hid behind a chair and covered his eyes.

"What's happening?" yelled Mother, as she raced into the room. "Let me see for myself!"

So Mom slowly bent down and carefully pulled back the spread.

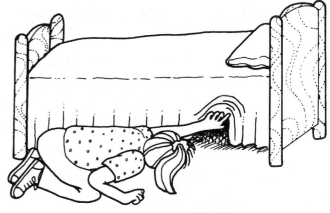

"Yes, Charlie, there really is a horrible monster under your bed, and you'd better get rid of it now!"

"Oh, it's you, little dustball," I said. "I guess you'll have to find a new home—maybe in my closet. But try to keep it a secret this time!"

Check the box that completes the sentence.

This story is about a boy who . . . ☐ needs to clean under his bed.

☐ collects monsters under his bed.

Color only the fuzzy monster words that describe the monster under Charlie's bed.

neat   noisy   cute   dirty   fuzzy

Draw a mouth on each person to show how each looked when he/she discovered the monster under Charlie's bed.

Amy   Kevin   Mom   Charlie

Extension: Write about a "monster" you keep under your bed at home.

Name _____

Too Much TV

Telly watched TV whenever he could. Every day he turned on the television as soon as he hopped out of the bed. When he came home from school, his right hand was on the remote control as soon as his left hand closed the door. Telly excused himself from dinner to secretly watch more TV. He even sat in front of the set while he did his homework.

One day something very strange happened. Telly's head started becoming square-shaped. Then, he grew a V-shaped antenna on the top of his head! Buttons and numbers appeared on his chest. Telly was turning into a TV!

Telly knew what he had to do. Each day he watched less and less TV. He played baseball, read books, and talked to his family members. He found there were lots more exciting things than TV.

Number the following pictures in the correct order.

Think about what you like to spend a lot of time doing. Write about what you might turn into.

_____

_____

_____

_____

Name _____

This Little Piggy . . .

Three little pigs left their mother to go to sea. When they couldn't agree on what kind of boat to build, each pig built his own.

The first pig planned to build his boat from straw, while the second pig chose sticks. They both laughed at the third pig when they saw him gathering bricks.

"Those bricks will sink, and you will get all wet!" laughed the two pigs.

When the three pigs were finished, they brought their boats to the river to test them.

The straw boat was not strong enough to hold the weight of the chubby pig, and the boat sank to the bottom.

The stick boat was not tied together well, and as water seeped in, it sank also.

The third pig floated happily down the river as the other pigs looked on in surprise.

"I put the bricks on top of a strong log raft," yelled the third pig to his brothers.

Check the boxes that describe each pig.

	boat builder	stubborn	careless	wet	clever
First Pig					
Second Pig					
Third Pig					

Circle the picture(s) which answer(s) each question correctly.

In the beginning, which pig(s) seemed to have the worst plan(s)?

 First Pig    Second Pig    Third Pig

In the end, which pig(s) seemed to have the worst plan(s)?

 First Pig    Second Pig    Third Pig

Name _____

Home Sweet Home

"You can't get me!" shouted Goldie as she smiled a crooked smile. She even managed to make a funny face while staring directly into his eyes.

"I don't want to play with you anyway!" answered Tom, knowing that Goldie was right. So he turned up his nose a bit and walked out of sight.

Although she used to be afraid of Tom, Goldie now liked to tease him. "It's fun to tease Tom because when he's upset, his hair stands up on his neck.

Soon Goldie could hear noises outside. Mom was home. "It is almost time for dinner," thought Goldie.

"I'm really glad to be a goldfish," sighed Goldie. "I'm safe and sound and very well fed!"

Draw a picture of Tom.

What clues in the story told you about Tom?

_____

_____

Complete the sentence below.

Goldie was glad to be a goldfish because . . .

_____

_____ .

Name _____

Grin and Bear It!

Hey, Winnie! Here comes a new group of people. Look at that man's funny, flowered shorts. I sure wouldn't want to be seen wearing them. That lady has a hat that would probably look better as a flower pot. A daisy could be growing from it.

They all just point and stare. It's too hot to be standing in the direct sun. I wonder how they cool off. I'm going to go swimming. Maybe they'll start throwing treats if I roll over and then sit up. Everyone loves that. Boy, do I have them trained!

Check all the boxes that show how bears and people are alike.

☐ wear shorts with flowers

☐ like to watch others

☐ can go swimming when it's hot

☐ eat fish

☐ do tricks for treats

Underline the correct answers.

Bears entertain people by . . .

• swimming

• wearing funny clothing

• rolling over and sitting up

People entertain the bears by . . .

• wearing funny hats

• throwing treats

• doing tricks for food

Name _____

The Investigation

The bowl sat empty. "Oh, no! My spaghetti is missing!" shrieked Mom. "I was supposed to take it to the school potluck tonight."

"Don't panic Mom, I'll look for clues." Hmmmm . . . The spaghetti had been in the bowl, on the counter, near the sink. First, I ran outside to check for footprints . . . None! It must have been an inside job.

Who would be my first suspect? I went to Baby Laurie's room. There was no sign of the spaghetti, not even on Baby Laurie.

Next, I asked Dad if he had seen anything unusual. He had been mowing the lawn and didn't know anything about the case.

My leads seemed to be vanishing. Could a thief have come into our house and helped himself to dinner? Had aliens zapped it aboard their spaceship?

I scratched my head and looked around. Suddenly, I noticed through the open window two birds carrying long, red-and-white worms in their beaks. The Case of the Missing Spaghetti is now closed!

Check the correct answers.

1. Baby Laurie did not take the spaghetti because she . . .

   ☐ did not like spaghetti.

   ☐ was too young.

   ☐ was not wearing any of it on her clothing.

2. Dad did not take the spaghetti because he . . .

   ☐ had been too busy mowing the lawn.

   ☐ had not seen anything.

   ☐ liked pizza better.

3. The birds probably took the spaghetti because they . . .

   ☐ liked Italian food.

   ☐ thought they were worms.

   ☐ wanted to try something different.

Name _____

The Cure

Mom is sick! The doctor says she needs to stay in bed all day. So I've decided to help her.

I will begin by cleaning the carpet where I spilled my grape juice when I bent over to pick up the peanut butter-and-jelly sandwich I had dropped earlier. The carpet is pretty sticky. Soooo, I think I'll bring the hose inside. One quick squirt should take care of that mess!

Boy, that was easy! Now I will help Mom wash clothes. Let's see . . . I bet if I use the whole box of soap, the clothes will get extra clean!

Now, while the clothes are washing, I'll fix Mom some lunch. Oops! That plate sure was slippery! Let's see.

Where does she keep the . . . What's that rumbling noise? Why is soap rushing from the laundry room? "Oh, that's you, Mom! You must be feeling better. You were supposed to stay in bed all day!"

Underline the correct answer to complete each sentence.

The rug became nice and clean and fluffy.
soaking wet.

The washing machine overflowed.
washed the clothes extra clean.

Mom probably enjoyed her child's lunch.
fixed her own lunch.

Circle Yes or No for each sentence.

The child tried to make a mess.	Yes	No
The child wants to help his mom.	Yes	No
Mom probably told her child to go out and play.	Yes	No

Extension: Draw a picture of yourself helping your mom when she is sick.

Name _____

A Royal Smile

"Braces! I have to wear braces!" exclaimed Arthur.

"That's right," answered Dr. Straight as he finished tightening the metal strips. "Your smile will be wonderful. Let's finish by adding purple bands."

On the way home, Arthur pouted and complained. "At school I will never talk again. I will shake or nod my head whenever anyone talks to me."

The next day Arthur did as he had planned. He nodded to the bus driver when she remarked that it was a beautiful day. He shook his head when his teacher asked if he had finished his homework. After a while, his head began to hurt from nodding and shaking it so much.

But things began to change during social studies. The class was learning about kings and queens. Mrs. Wise said that purple was a royal color.

"Hmmm," thought Arthur. "Maybe with my purple and silver teeth I am related to a king," and he began to smile a big, toothy grin. His friends noticed his braces.

"Cool," said Lance. "I hope I will get braces, someday. I'd like all different colors on my teeth."

"Purple is sooo grand," said Gwen.

Draw a 😊 if it's a good idea.

Draw a 🙁 if it's a bad idea.

◯ Dr. Straight put braces on Arthur's teeth.

◯ Arthur pouted and complained about getting braces.

◯ Arthur wouldn't talk at school.

◯ Arthur smiled when he learned purple was a royal color.

◯ Arthur's friends thought his braces were cool.

Rearrange the letters in the word **smile** and write the new word on the braces to answer the following question:
How much happiness is in a smile?

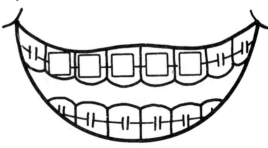

Name _____

That's a Pizza!

Papa Luigi is having a bad day. He forgot to order some things that he uses to make his very special pizza.

Pete walked into the restaurant. "I'd like to order your 'Papa Luigi's Pizza Supremo'," he stated.

"I'm sorry, but I do not have all of the toppings," explained Papa Luigi. "However, I will make one large sur-prise pizza at a special price of $5.00."

"Okay," said Pete.

"Pizza good sport!" thought Luigi.

Use the clues to find what toppings were on the pizza.

1. __ __ __ __ __ __ (rhymes with sneeze)

2. __ __ __ ato (Thomas' nickname)

3. saus __ __ __ (the number of years one has lived)

4. pine __ __ __ __ __ (a red fruit)

5. o __ __ __ __ s (opposite of die)

Now discover what toppings were missing.

1. mush __ __ __ __ __ (areas in a house)

2. __ __ __ __ __ peppers ("go" on a stoplight)

3. g __ __ __ __ __ beef (shape of a circle)

4. __ __ __ __ __ __ oni (opposite of salt)

5. __ __ i __ __ s (opposite of off—twice)

The Inventor

Every day after school, Bert came home and locked himself in his bedroom. He was working on a secret project.

After three months Bert was finished. He had made a robot that looked exactly like himself. The robot even had orange hair, freckles, and glasses. The robot talked in a squeaky voice just like Bert and giggled when its toes were tickled. "Life is going to be easy now!" exclaimed Bert. "I'm going to send my robot to school while I stay home and play."

The next morning the robot ate breakfast, rode the bus, and went to school. After school the bus dropped the robot back home. The robot knocked on the door.

"Sweetie, I am so glad you're home. I really missed you!" said Mom, as she kissed the robot on the forehead. Then she took the robot into the kitchen and gave him a snack before dinner.

"We had lots of fun at school today," said the robot. "We went to the space museum and learned about astronauts."

Bert decided that maybe this wasn't such a great idea. So the next day, Bert went to school himself.

Draw a line from each group of words to the correct picture(s).

has orange hair, freckles, and glasses

thinks with a brain

goes to school

has a squeaky voice

is a machine

wants someone to do his work

Check the correct answer to the question.

What lesson did Bert learn?

☐ A robot can't do everything for you.　　☐ Missing school is always fun.

Extension: What would you have a robot do for you? _____

Name _____

The Kiss

Once upon a time a pretty princess walked to a pond in the castle forest. She took off her shoes and socks and stepped into the cool water. Just then a green frog jumped off a lily pad and startled the princess. She began to cry.

"I am sorry, little princess. I didn't mean to frighten you," apologized the frog. "What can I do to make you feel better?"

The little princess sat down on the grass, shrugged her shoulders, and kept crying.

Finally, the frog hopped up on a rock and kissed her cheek. Magically, the princess changed into a little green frog!

"Thank-you, kind frog," said the princess. "Now the magic spell is broken. I am a frog once again and can live by this beautiful pond forever."

Draw a 🌿 above the words that describe the frog. Draw a 👑 above the words that describe the princess.

unhappy	sorry	thankful
frightened	kind to strangers	under a magic spell

Check the correct answer to the question.

What really made the little princess cry?

☐ She wanted to be a frog again.   ☐ She was scared of the frog.

Name _____

My Haunted House

I know that our house is haunted, but I still get blamed for everything that goes wrong! I pick up my toys when I'm finished playing, but Dad always seems to be tripping over one of them. I hang my clothes in the closet, but Mom says she finds them all over the floor. Even my big sister accuses me of getting into her things. I would never do that or any of the other things I'm blamed for. Why is that ghost trying to get me in trouble?

Read what it says under each window in the house. Draw a face in the window that states the main idea. Draw a ghost in all of the windows that are supporting details.

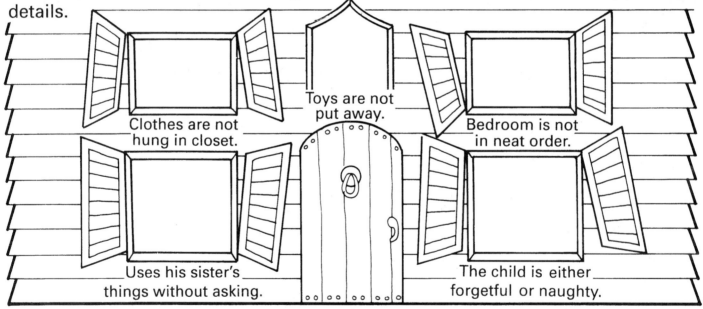

Clothes are not hung in closet.

Toys are not put away.

Bedroom is not in neat order.

Uses his sister's things without asking.

The child is either forgetful or naughty.

Rewrite the main idea sentence from the windows above to help the child solve the problem.

_____

Extension: Write two ways the "ghost" in your house gets you in trouble.

1. _____

2. _____

Name _____

Time Machine

It is finally finished! The world's first portable, one-seater time machine is ready for action! Because I am the inventor, I will bravely take the test ride. My brother Albert will record all of the results.

First, I must push button #1 and slide the red lever into the "go" slot. Next, I will turn button #2 to the left and pull on the green handle. This is it! After I push button #3 two times, I will be ready to launch!

What a trip this is—lights speeding toward me from all directions! It is hard to see what is in front of me! I'm racing into the future.

Oooooh! What happened? I've come to a complete stop! I'd better get out and investigate.

Dad is here in the future, and he looks angry. Seems he can't find his tools. And there's Mom; she's yelling, "What's happened to this room!"

Uh, oh! Maybe I'd better go back in time and pick up a few things before I go for another ride!

Circle the correct answers.

What things did the inventor need to pick up?

Dad's tools   a barbell   messy room   the mail   his time machine

Where do you think the inventor was?

_____

_____

Match the phrases by writing the letter of the correct answer on each line.

If the inventor traveled to the future and returned home, this would help him . . .

____ do his homework

____ be a reporter

____ understand a story

____ be a detective

a. because he would already know the ending.

b. because he would know who was guilty.

c. because he would already know the answers.

d. because he would already know the news.

Name _____

Mind Game

One afternoon Samantha sat with her friends on their front steps. She began to brag that she could read their minds. She put her hands on Maria's head, closed her eyes, and said, "You had red punch with your lunch!"

"Wow! You're right!" replied Maria, not realizing that she had a slightly red ring around her lips.

"If you're so smart, Samantha, then tell me what I just ate, because I bet I can read minds as well as you," sneered Thomas.

"That's a bunch of baloney," answered Samantha.

"How did you know!" asked Thomas.

"It's my little secret," said Samantha, giving a sigh of relief.

"Here comes your mom," said Maria. "Can you read her mind, too?"

Samantha looked down at her watch. She should have been home a half hour ago. As she took off running, she yelled, "Yes, I know exactly what she's thinking!"

Underline the correct answer.

1. Samantha knew that Maria had red punch because . . .

   Maria always drinks red punch.   Maria had a red ring around her lips.

2. Samantha said that Thomas had eaten baloney because . . .

   she made a lucky guess.   baloney tastes good.

3. Samanatha read her mother's mind because . . .

   she had special powers.   she knew she was late.

Circle the correct answer.

1. If a boy has fur all over his clothes, he probably . . .   has a pet.

   likes fluffy clothes.

2. If a girl has a blue tongue, she probably . . .   is very sick.

   just ate a blueberry Popsicle.

3. If a man always wears a baseball cap, . . .   his head is probably cold.

   he probably just likes hats.

Name _____

Bath-Time Blues

"I hate baths!" Zack cried as his mother pointed to the bathroom.

"If you are smelly and dirty, no one will come near you," Mother said calmly.

"I don't care, I still hate baths!" Zack yelled, as he went running through the house.

When Zack's mother finally caught him and carried him into the bathroom, Zack knew there was no escape.

Mother closed the door and called, "Have fun!"

Zack pretended his rubber fish was a shark. He put it into the water and made creepy noises. Then Zack yelled "It's got my toes, Mom! It's pulling me under! I'd better get out quick!"

"Keep scrubbing," called Mother.

When Zack used the soap and brush to scrub the dirt away he shouted, "My skin is falling off!"

"Keep scrubbing," Mom answered once again.

When Zack's bath time was over, he dried himself, combed his hair, and got dressed in clean clothes.

"You smell so sweet, and you look so handsome," she replied.

"Thanks!" said Zack as he rushed outside to play in the dirt.

Find the Word Bank words across and down in the wordsearch.

Word Bank

loving	dirty
naughty	loud
quiet	calm
firm	wild

l	m	a	b	e	j	w	y
o	s	t	e	a	d	o	b
v	e	k	f	w	i	l	d
i	z	q	f	i	r	m	c
n	a	u	g	h	t	y	a
g	b	i	d	a	y	e	l
t	h	e	l	o	u	d	m
p	u	t	m	r	g	a	h

Circle the four words that describe Zack, blue. Circle the four words that describe his mom, red.

Answer Key
Reading Comprehension
Grade 2

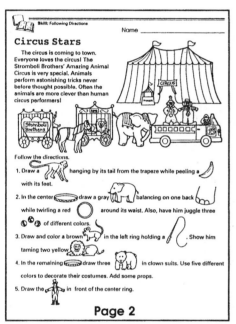

Skill: Following Directions

Circus Stars

The circus is coming to town. Everyone loves the circus! The Stromboli Brothers' Amazing Animal Circus is very special. Animals perform astonishing tricks never before thought possible. Often the animals are more clever than human circus performers!

Follow the directions.

1. Draw a ___ hanging by its tail from the trapeze while peeling a ___ with its feet.
2. In the center ___ draw a gray ___ balancing on one back ___ while twirling a red ___ around its waist. Also, have him juggle three ___ of different colors.
3. Draw and color a brown ___ in the left ring holding a ___. Show him taming two yellow ___.
4. In the remaining ___ draw three ___ in clown suits. Use five different colors to decorate their costumes. Add some props.
5. Draw the ___ in front of the center ring.

Page 2

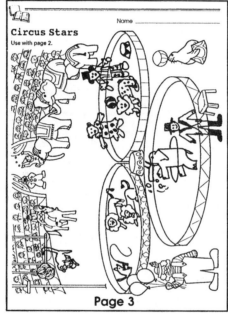

Circus Stars

Use with page 2.

Page 3

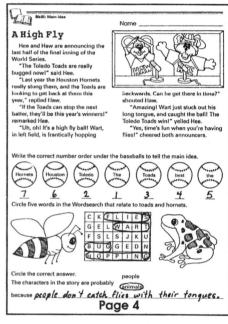

Skill: Main Idea

A High Fly

Hee and Haw are announcing the last half of the final inning of the World Series.

"The Toledo Toads are really bugged now!" said Hee.

"Last year the Houston Hornets really stung them, and the Toads are looking to get back at them this year," replied Haw.

"If the Toads can stop the next batter, they'll be this year's winners!" remarked Hee.

"Uh, oh! It's a high fly ball! Wart, in left field, is frantically hopping backwards. Can he get there in time?" shouted Haw.

"Amazing! Wart just stuck out his long tongue, and caught the ball! The Toledo Toads win!" yelled Hee.

"Yes, time's fun when you're having flies!" cheered both announcers.

Write the correct number order under the baseballs to tell the main idea.

Hornets	Houston	Toledo	The	Toads	best	the
7	6	2	1	3	4	5

Circle five words in the Wordsearch that relate to toads and hornets.

Circle the correct answer.
The characters in the story are probably (animals) [people]
because *people don't catch flies with their tongues.*

Page 4

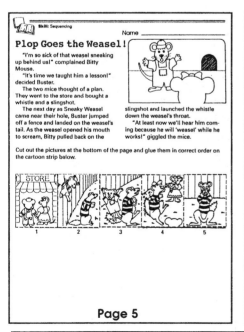

Skill: Sequencing

Plop Goes the Weasel!

"I'm so sick of that weasel sneaking up behind us!" complained Bitty Mouse.

"It's time we taught him a lesson!" decided Buster.

The two mice thought of a plan. They went to the store and bought a whistle and a slingshot.

The next day as Sneaky Weasel came near their hole, Buster jumped off a fence and landed on the weasel's tail. As the weasel opened his mouth to scream, Bitty pulled back on the slingshot and launched the whistle down the weasel's throat.

"At least now we'll hear him coming because he will 'weasel' while he works!" giggled the mice.

Cut out the pictures at the bottom of the page and glue them in correct order on the cartoon strip below.

Page 5

Skill: Character Analysis

The Cat's Meow

Sometimes Leo acts so strange! Two weeks ago he thought he was a duck. All day long he walked around wearing flippers on his feet and flapping his arms. When asked what he wanted for lunch, he answered, "Quack-ers, quack-ers." Last week he claimed to be a lightning bug. He even tied a light bulb on his back. When I asked him why he didn't light up, he said that his batteries must be run down. Well, today he thinks he's a cat. He has been purring since breakfast which, of course, was a bowl of milk. I warned him to stop jumping off the back of the couch. He says he doesn't need to worry because he has nine lives. Hmmm . . . I wonder how he'll like his dinner tonight? I have a little rubber mouse, and . . .

Unscramble the letters to write the name of the correct animal.

1. If Leo walks around shaking a rattle, he probably thinks he's a
   rattlesnake (kaltsnetrae)
2. If Leo paints black and white stripes all over himself, he probably thinks he's a
   zebra (arebz)
3. If Leo gobbles his food and sticks feathers in his clothes, he probably thinks he's a **turkey** (etkyu).
4. If Leo wears a sweatshirt with one large front pocket and hops around, he probably thinks he's a **kangaroo** (gaoknroa)

Extension: What might Leo do if he thought he were . . .
a dog? *Answers will vary.*
a bunny? *Answers will vary.*

Page 6

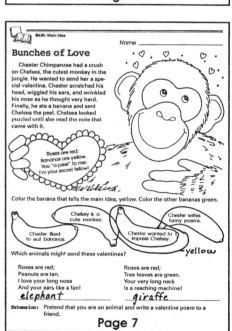

Skill: Main Idea

Bunches of Love

Chester Chimpanzee had a crush on Chelsea, the cutest monkey in the jungle. He wanted to send her a special valentine. Chester scratched his head, wiggled his ears, and wrinkled his nose as he thought very hard. Finally, he ate a banana and sent Chelsea the peel. Chelsea looked puzzled until she read the note that came with it.

Roses are red;
Bananas are yellow.
You "a-peel" to me!
I'm your secret fellow!

Color the banana that tells the main idea, yellow. Color the other bananas green.

Chelsey is a cute monkey.
Chester writes funny poems.
Chester liked to eat bananas.
Chester wanted to impress Chelsey. **yellow**

Which animals might send these valentines?

Roses are red;
Peanuts are tan.
I love your long nose
And your ears like a fan!
elephant

Roses are red;
Tree leaves are green.
Your very long neck
Is a reaching machine!
giraffe

Extension: Pretend that you are an animal and write a valentine poem to a friend.

Page 7

Page 8

Skill: Recognizing Details

Name _____

A Lot of Hot Air

Patrick bought fifteen sticks of bubble gum for the price of ten. He began putting the gum into his mouth. One, two, three pieces fit easily. Chomp! Chomp! Four, five, six were next. Chew! Chew! Seven, eight, nine, and so on, until all fifteen pieces filled his mouth. After a few small practice bubbles, Patrick decided that he would try to blow the biggest bubble ever. Slowly, he filled the bubble with air. It grew and grew until he tipped his head back and blew one huge puff of air.

Just then, something happened! Patrick felt his feet slowly lift off the ground. He looked from side to side and noticed he was staring at the tops of trees. He looked down and saw the top of his house.

A few moments later a tiny bluebird landed on top of the bubble. As the bird pecked at the bubble, its beak poked a hole in the bubble, and whoosh! Patrick began floating down to the ground. Luckily, he landed on top of a haystack. As he slid down, he thought to himself, "Next time, maybe fourteen pieces would be safer!"

Circle the correct word to complete each sentence.

Patrick chewed ~~ten~~ (fifteen) pieces of bubble gum.

A huge (bubble) ~~wind~~ lifted Patrick off the ground.

Patrick saw the tops of (trees and his house) ~~mountains~~.

A ~~haystack~~ (bird) popped Patrick's bubble.

Extension: Pretend you are above looking down. Draw the top of . . .

a boat.   a snowman.   an elephant.

Page 9

Skill: Cause and Effect

Name _____

Magic Wishes

Four animals found a magic lamp. They rubbed the lamp, and a genie appeared.

"I will grant each of you one wish," announced the genie.

"Make my trunk smaller!" demanded the vain elephant. "I wish to be the most beautiful elephant that ever lived."

"Make my legs longer!" commanded the alligator. "I want to be taller than all of my alligator friends."

"Make my neck shorter!" ordered the giraffe. "I am tired of always staring at the tops of trees."

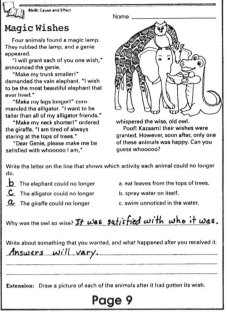

"Dear Genie, please make me be satisfied with whooooo I am,"

whispered the wise, old owl.

Poof! Kazaam! their wishes were granted. However, soon after, only one of these animals was happy. Can you guess whooooo?

Write the letter on the line that shows which activity each animal could no longer do.

b The elephant could no longer   a. eat leaves from the tops of trees.

c The alligator could no longer   b. spray water on itself.

a The giraffe could no longer   c. swim unnoticed in the water.

Why was the owl so wise? _It was satisfied with who it was._

Write about something that you wanted, and what happened after you received it.
Answers will vary.
_____

Extension: Draw a picture of each of the animals after it had gotten its wish.

Page 10

Skill: Classification

Name _____

Going for a Ride

Welcome to the Amazing Adventure Theme Park! This park has many exciting new rides.

Use the Word Bank to write the name of each ride that fits in the boxes below. All names will be written across → .

Word Bank		
Aladdin's Lamp	Magic Carpet	Comet Crash
Sea Kingdom	Crater Dip	Glass Slipper
Meteor Bumper	Monster Mash	Tilt-a-Whirlpool
Ride-the-Waves	Make-a-Splash	Flying Saucers
	Big Dipper	

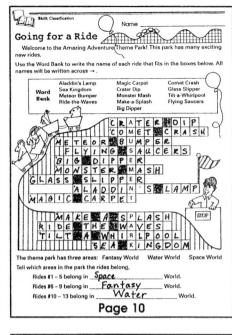

CRATER DIP
COMET CRASH
METEOR BUMPER
FLYING SAUCERS
BIG DIPPER
MONSTER MASH
GLASS SLIPPER
ALADDIN'S LAMP
MAGIC CARPET

MAKE A SPLASH
RIDE THE WAVES
TILT A WHIRLPOOL
SEA KINGDOM

The theme park has three areas: Fantasy World   Water World   Space World

Tell which areas in the park the rides belong.

Rides #1 – 5 belong in _Space_ World.

Rides #6 – 9 belong in _Fantasy_ World.

Rides #10 – 13 belong in _Water_ World.

Page 11

Skill: Predicting Outcomes

Name _____

Itsy, Bitsy Spider

One sunny afternoon Stan and Ollie were chasing each other around the yard. After a while, they both grew tired and decided to rest in the grass. As they rested, the boys noticed a tiny spider begin to climb into a drain spout.

"You know about the itsy, bitsy spider don't you?" asked Ollie. "Let's see what will happen."

"I'll get the hose and squirt water into the top of the gutter. You watch

from the bottom and see if the spider comes down," suggested Stan.

So, Stan turned on the hose and aimed it at the top of the gutter . . .

Tell what you think happened next. _Answers will vary._
_____

Draw an escape plan for the spider. Include all of the characters from the story. Label the parts.

Pictures will vary.

Page 12

Skill: Inference

Name _____

Digging for Treasure

Petey and I decided to dig for buried treasure. I wasn't sure where to start, but Petey had a feeling that we should dig behind the big oak tree. So that is what we did.

We dug for hours. Our pile of dirt was growing taller by the minute. Suddenly my shovel hit something hard. Petey and I became excited, and our hearts began thumping. We dug faster and faster. Soon, we had uncovered what seemed to be a gigantic bone! Maybe it had belonged to a dinosaur! I imagined bringing it to a museum and receiving an award. I turned to tell Petey about my thoughts, but when I looked around, he and the bone were gone!

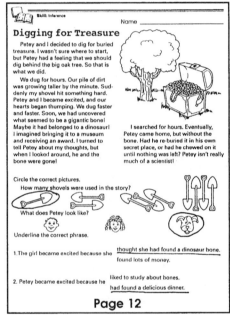

I searched for hours. Eventually, Petey came home, but without the bone. Had he re-buried it in his own secret place, or had he chewed on it until nothing was left? Petey isn't really much of a scientist!

Circle the correct pictures.

How many shovels were used in the story?

What does Petey look like?

Underline the correct phrase.

1. The girl became excited because she __thought she had found a dinosaur bone__ / found lots of money.

2. Petey became excited because he liked to study about bones. / __had found a delicious dinner.__

Page 13

Skill: Inference

Name _____

Digging for Treasure

Use with page 12.

Use the Word Bank and the riddles to write what kind of bones Petey and his friend discovered on later "digs."

Word Bank	
lamb	cow
chicken	mouse
porcupine	squirrel

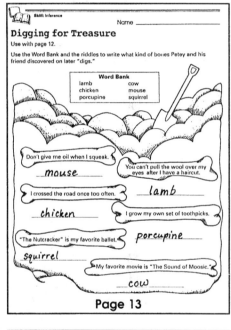

Don't give me oil when I squeak. _mouse_

You can't pull the wool over my eyes after I have a haircut. _lamb_

I crossed the road once too often. _chicken_

I grow my own set of toothpicks. _porcupine_

"The Nutcracker" is my favorite ballet. _squirrel_

My favorite movie is "The Sound of Moosic." _cow_

Page 14

Skill: Evaluation

Name _____

The Perfect Excuse

"I don't see your homework," announced Mrs. Crabtree.

"Don't you see my paper?" I answered. "I put it on your desk."

"All I see is a blank sheet of paper," she said.

"Wow! Then it must have really happened! Last night when I sat down to do my homework, I thought I saw two giggling ghosts fly into my bedroom. They offered me 'ghoul-aid,' and I drank a full cup. All of a sudden my toes and legs disappeared! Before I could yell out, my whole body had become invisible!

"Oh, really!" said Mrs. Crabtree, looking confused.

"However, Mrs. Crabtree, I know I had homework to finish, so I kept on

writing after they left."

"And then what happened?" asked Mrs. Crabtree.

"When I woke up this morning, I was happy to see that I was no longer invisible! My homework is proof that this really happened! Those silly ghosts must have given me invisible ink to write with!"

Write the good habits in the heart and the bad habits in the ghost.

doing homework	telling lies	making excuses
being lazy	being honest	listening carefully

Heart: _doing homework, being honest, listening carefully_

Ghost: _being lazy, telling lies, making excuses_

Circle and write.

Mrs. Crabtree ~~did~~ (did not) believe the student's story because _she does not believe in ghosts._

Page 15

Skill: Recognizing Details

Name _____

What's Up, Doc?

"Open wide!" ordered Dr. Allswell. "I want to check your tonsils."

The patient did exactly as he was told. The doctor sprayed the animal's throat with medication. "Your sore throat should feel better by tomorrow," said the doctor.

The next patient hobbled into the office.

"I can see that your knees are swollen. I'll wrap them and give you medicine to help get rid of the pain, but please try to lose a little weight. Carrying too many extra pounds can make your legs cramp and feel sore."

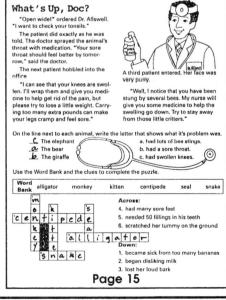

A third patient entered. Her face was very puffy.

"Well, I notice that you have been stung by several bees. My nurse will give you some medicine to help the swelling go down. Try to stay away from those little critters."

On the line next to each animal, write the letter that shows what its problem was.

c The elephant   a. had lots of bee stings.

a The bear   b. had a sore throat.

b The giraffe   c. had swollen knees.

Use the Word Bank and the clues to complete the puzzle.

Word Bank	alligator	monkey	kitten	centipede	seal	snake

Across:
4. had many sore feet
5. needed 50 fillings in his teeth
6. scratched her tummy on the ground

Down:
1. became sick from too many bananas
2. began disliking milk
3. lost her loud bark

Crossword:
centipede
alligator
snake

Page 16

Skill: Sequencing

Name _____

A Hare-Raising Experience

Jack Rabbit loved to grow carrots. First, he found a diamond-shaped field. Next, he carefully planted and watered the seeds. Then, he watched as the little green tops of carrots began pushing through the dirt. Finally, 83 carrots were ready to be pulled from the earth. Jack indeed had his 83 "carrot" diamond in town, and he proudly gave it to his friend Jill.

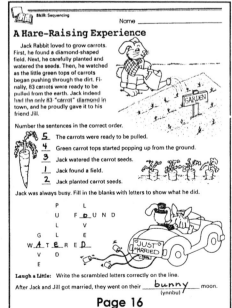

Number the sentences in the correct order.

5 The carrots were ready to be pulled.

4 Green carrot tops started popping up from the ground.

3 Jack watered the carrot seeds.

1 Jack found a field.

2 Jack planted carrot seeds.

Jack was always busy. Fill in the blanks with letters to show what he did.

PULLED
FOUND
WATERED

Laugh a Little: Write the scrambled letters correctly on the line.

After Jack and Jill got married, they went on their _bunny_ (ynnbu) moon.

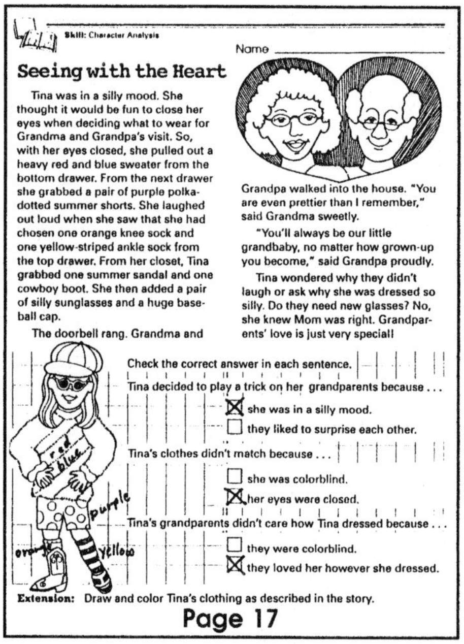

Skill: Character Analysis

Name ______

Seeing with the Heart

Tina was in a silly mood. She thought it would be fun to close her eyes when deciding what to wear for Grandma and Grandpa's visit. So, with her eyes closed, she pulled out a heavy red and blue sweater from the bottom drawer. From the next drawer she grabbed a pair of purple polka-dotted summer shorts. She laughed out loud when she saw that she had chosen one orange knee sock and one yellow-striped ankle sock from the top drawer. From her closet, Tina grabbed one summer sandal and one cowboy boot. She then added a pair of silly sunglasses and a huge baseball cap.

The doorbell rang. Grandma and Grandpa walked into the house. "You are even prettier than I remember," said Grandma sweetly.

"You'll always be our little grandbaby, no matter how grown-up you become," said Grandpa proudly.

Tina wondered why they didn't laugh or ask why she was dressed so silly. Do they need new glasses? No, she knew Mom was right. Grandparents' love is just very special!

Check the correct answer in each sentence.

Tina decided to play a trick on her grandparents because . . .

- [x] she was in a silly mood.
- [ ] they liked to surprise each other.

Tina's clothes didn't match because . . .

- [ ] she was colorblind.
- [x] her eyes were closed.

Tina's grandparents didn't care how Tina dressed because . . .

- [ ] they were colorblind.
- [x] they loved her however she dressed.

Extension: Draw and color Tina's clothing as described in the story.

Page 17

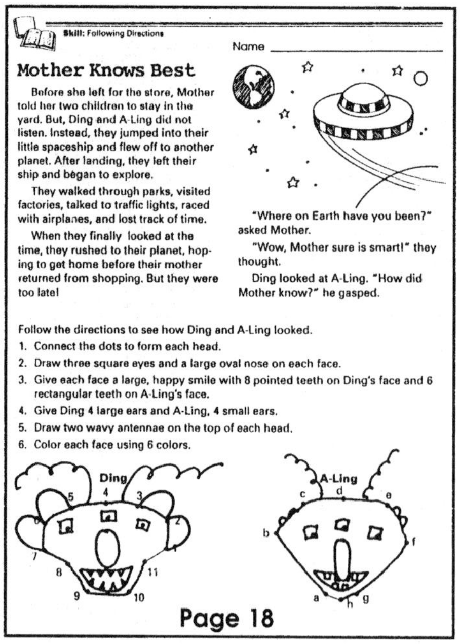

Skill: Following Directions

Name ______

Mother Knows Best

Before she left for the store, Mother told her two children to stay in the yard. But, Ding and A-Ling did not listen. Instead, they jumped into their little spaceship and flew off to another planet. After landing, they left their ship and began to explore.

They walked through parks, visited factories, talked to traffic lights, raced with airplanes, and lost track of time.

When they finally looked at the time, they rushed to their planet, hoping to get home before their mother returned from shopping. But they were too late!

"Where on Earth have you been?" asked Mother.

"Wow, Mother sure is smart!" they thought.

Ding looked at A-Ling. "How did Mother know?" he gasped.

Follow the directions to see how Ding and A-Ling looked.

1. Connect the dots to form each head.
2. Draw three square eyes and a large oval nose on each face.
3. Give each face a large, happy smile with 8 pointed teeth on Ding's face and 6 rectangular teeth on A-Ling's face.
4. Give Ding 4 large ears and A-Ling, 4 small ears.
5. Draw two wavy antennae on the top of each head.
6. Color each face using 6 colors.

Page 18

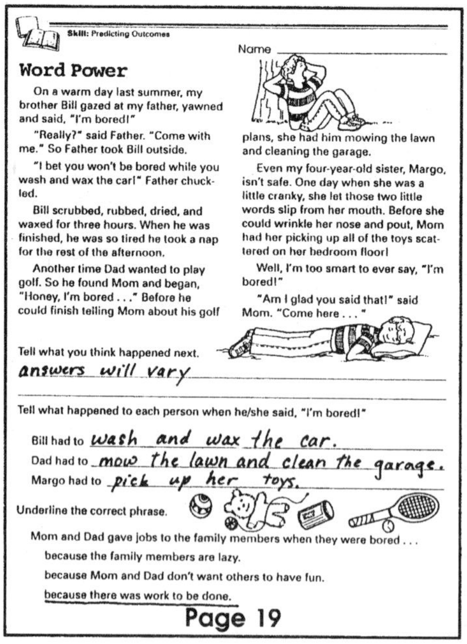

Skill: Predicting Outcomes

Name ______

Word Power

On a warm day last summer, my brother Bill gazed at my father, yawned and said, "I'm bored!"

"Really?" said Father. "Come with me." So Father took Bill outside.

"I bet you won't be bored while you wash and wax the car!" Father chuckled.

Bill scrubbed, rubbed, dried, and waxed for three hours. When he was finished, he was so tired he took a nap for the rest of the afternoon.

Another time Dad wanted to play golf. So he found Mom and began, "Honey, I'm bored . . ." Before he could finish telling Mom about his golf plans, she had him mowing the lawn and cleaning the garage.

Even my four-year-old sister, Margo, isn't safe. One day when she was a little cranky, she let those two little words slip from her mouth. Before she could wrinkle her nose and pout, Mom had her picking up all of the toys scattered on her bedroom floor!

Well, I'm too smart to ever say, "I'm bored!"

"Am I glad you said that!" said Mom. "Come here . . ."

Tell what you think happened next.

answers will vary

Tell what happened to each person when he/she said, "I'm bored!"

Bill had to *wash and wax the car.*

Dad had to *mow the lawn and clean the garage.*

Margo had to *pick up her toys.*

Underline the correct phrase.

Mom and Dad gave jobs to the family members when they were bored . . .

because the family members are lazy.

because Mom and Dad don't want others to have fun.

<u>because there was work to be done.</u>

Page 19

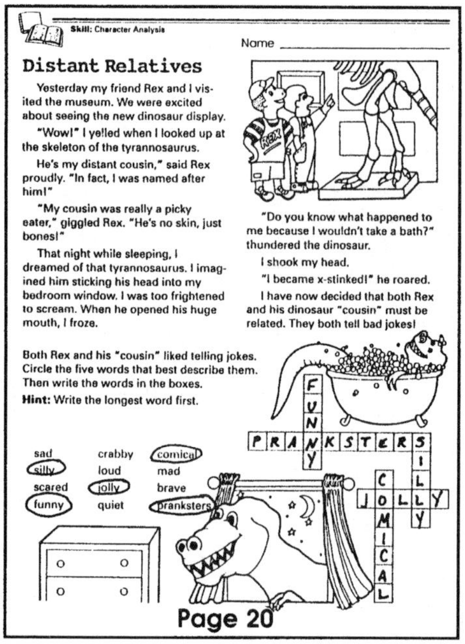

Skill: Character Analysis

Name ______

Distant Relatives

Yesterday my friend Rex and I visited the museum. We were excited about seeing the new dinosaur display.

"Wow!" I yelled when I looked up at the skeleton of the tyrannosaurus.

He's my distant cousin," said Rex proudly. "In fact, I was named after him!"

"My cousin was really a picky eater," giggled Rex. "He's no skin, just bones!"

That night while sleeping, I dreamed of that tyrannosaurus. I imagined him sticking his head into my bedroom window. I was too frightened to scream. When he opened his huge mouth, I froze.

"Do you know what happened to me because I wouldn't take a bath?" thundered the dinosaur.

I shook my head.

"I became x-stinked!" he roared.

I have now decided that both Rex and his dinosaur "cousin" must be related. They both tell bad jokes!

Both Rex and his "cousin" liked telling jokes. Circle the five words that best describe them. Then write the words in the boxes.

Hint: Write the longest word first.

sad, crabby, (comical), (silly), loud, mad, scared, (jolly), brave, (funny), quiet, (pranksters)

Page 20

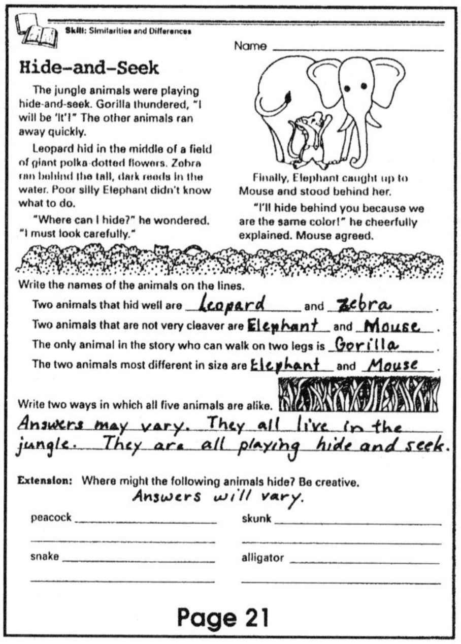

Skill: Similarities and Differences

Name ______

Hide-and-Seek

The jungle animals were playing hide-and-seek. Gorilla thundered, "I will be 'It'!" The other animals ran away quickly.

Leopard hid in the middle of a field of giant polka dotted flowers. Zebra ran behind the tall, dark reeds in the water. Poor silly Elephant didn't know what to do.

"Where can I hide?" he wondered. "I must look carefully."

Finally, Elephant caught up to Mouse and stood behind her.

"I'll hide behind you because we are the same color!" he cheerfully explained. Mouse agreed.

Write the names of the animals on the lines.

Two animals that hid well are *Leopard* and *Zebra*.

Two animals that are not very cleaver are *Elephant* and *Mouse*.

The only animal in the story who can walk on two legs is *Gorilla*.

The two animals most different in size are *Elephant* and *Mouse*.

Write two ways in which all five animals are alike.

Answers may vary. They all live in the jungle. They are all playing hide and seek.

Extension: Where might the following animals hide? Be creative.

Answers will vary.

peacock ______ skunk ______

snake ______ alligator ______

Page 21

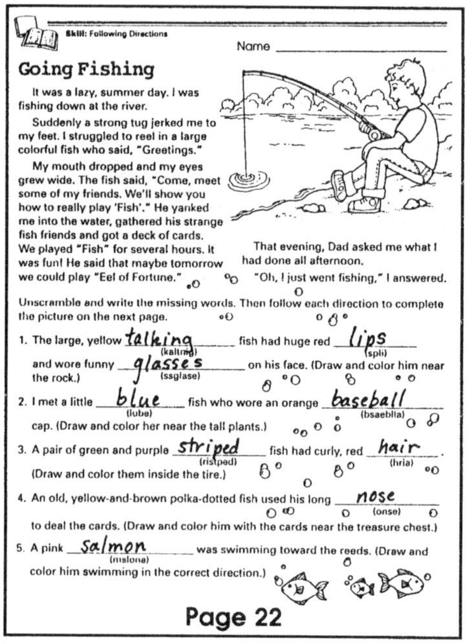

Skill: Following Directions

Name ______

Going Fishing

It was a lazy, summer day. I was fishing down at the river.

Suddenly a strong tug jerked me to my feet. I struggled to reel in a large colorful fish who said, "Greetings."

My mouth dropped and my eyes grew wide. The fish said, "Come, meet some of my friends. We'll show you how to really play 'Fish'." He yanked me into the water, gathered his strange fish friends and got a deck of cards. We played "Fish" for several hours. It was fun! He said that maybe tomorrow we could play "Eel of Fortune."

That evening, Dad asked me what I had done all afternoon.

"Oh, I just went fishing," I answered.

Unscramble and write the missing words. Then follow each direction to complete the picture on the next page.

1. The large, yellow *talking* (kaltingk) fish had huge red *lips* (spli) and wore funny *glasses* (ssglase) on his face. (Draw and color him near the rock.)
2. I met a little *blue* (lube) fish who wore an orange *baseball* (bsaeblla) cap. (Draw and color her near the tall plants.)
3. A pair of green and purple *striped* (ristped) fish had curly, red *hair* (hria). (Draw and color them inside the tire.)
4. An old, yellow-and-brown polka-dotted fish used his long *nose* (onse) to deal the cards. (Draw and color him with the cards near the treasure chest.)
5. A pink *salmon* (mlsona) was swimming toward the reeds. (Draw and color him swimming in the correct direction.)

Page 22

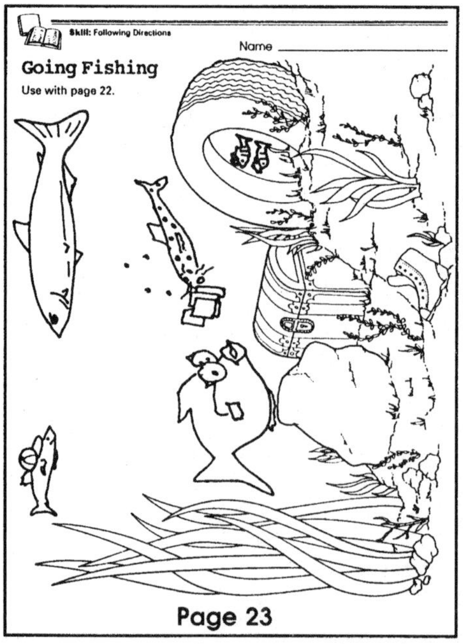

Skill: Following Directions

Name ______

Going Fishing

Use with page 22.

Page 23

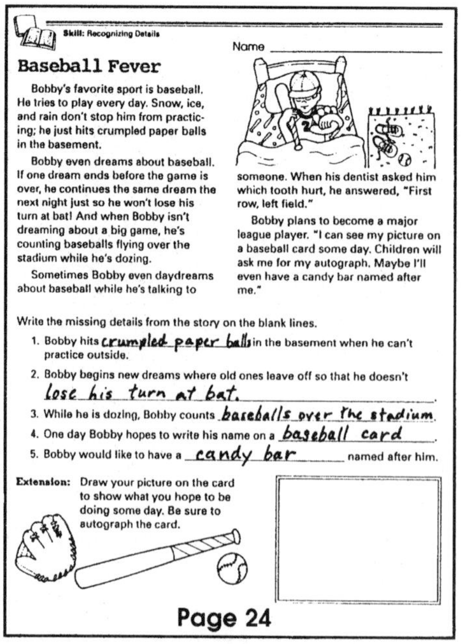

Skill: Recognizing Details

Name ______

Baseball Fever

Bobby's favorite sport is baseball. He tries to play every day. Snow, ice, and rain don't stop him from practicing; he just hits crumpled paper balls in the basement.

Bobby even dreams about baseball. If one dream ends before the game is over, he continues the same dream the next night just so he won't lose his turn at bat! And when Bobby isn't dreaming about a big game, he's counting baseballs flying over the stadium while he's dozing.

Sometimes Bobby even daydreams about baseball while he's talking to someone. When his dentist asked him which tooth hurt, he answered, "First row, left field."

Bobby plans to become a major league player. "I can see my picture on a baseball card some day. Children will ask me for my autograph. Maybe I'll even have a candy bar named after me."

Write the missing details from the story on the blank lines.

1. Bobby hits *crumpled paper balls* in the basement when he can't practice outside.
2. Bobby begins new dreams where old ones leave off so that he doesn't *lose his turn at bat.*
3. While he is dozing, Bobby counts *baseballs over the stadium*.
4. One day Bobby hopes to write his name on a *baseball card*.
5. Bobby would like to have a *candy bar* named after him.

Extension: Draw your picture on the card to show what you hope to be doing some day. Be sure to autograph the card.

Page 24

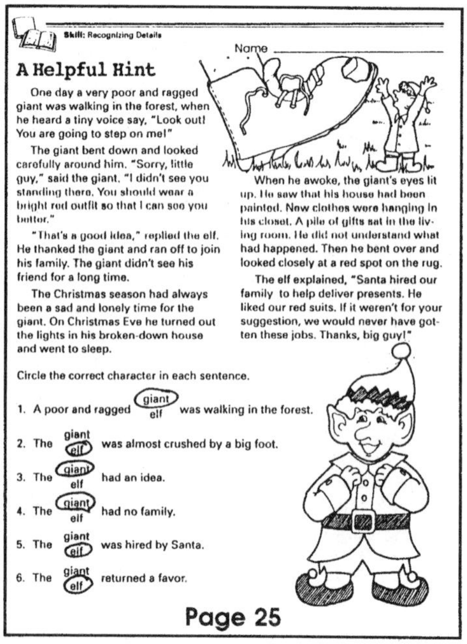

Skill: Recognizing Details

Name ______

A Helpful Hint

One day a very poor and ragged giant was walking in the forest, when he heard a tiny voice say, "Look out! You are going to step on me!"

The giant bent down and looked carefully around him. "Sorry, little guy," said the giant. "I didn't see you standing there. You should wear a bright red outfit so that I can see you better."

"That's a good idea," replied the elf. He thanked the giant and ran off to join his family. The giant didn't see his friend for a long time.

The Christmas season had always been a sad and lonely time for the giant. On Christmas Eve he turned out the lights in his broken-down house and went to sleep.

When he awoke, the giant's eyes lit up. He saw that his house had been painted. New clothes were hanging in his closet. A pile of gifts sat in the living room. He did not understand what had happened. Then he bent over and looked closely at a red spot on the rug.

The elf explained, "Santa hired our family to help deliver presents. He liked our red suits. If it weren't for your suggestion, we would never have gotten these jobs. Thanks, big guy!"

Circle the correct character in each sentence.

1. A poor and ragged (giant) / elf was walking in the forest.
2. The giant / (elf) was almost crushed by a big foot.
3. The (giant) / elf had an idea.
4. The (giant) / elf had no family.
5. The giant / (elf) was hired by Santa.
6. The giant / (elf) returned a favor.

Page 25

Skill: Sequencing

Name ____________

What a Mouthful!

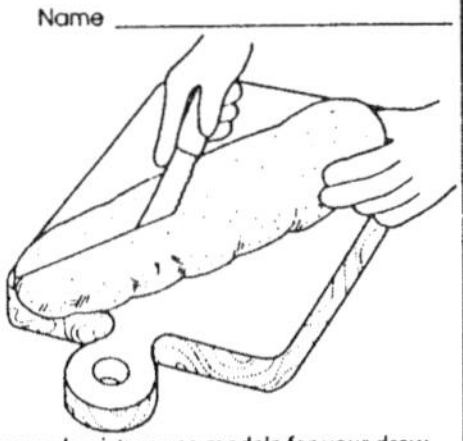

Clark wanted to make a super sandwich. He gathered food from the cupboards and refrigerator. First, he sliced a long loaf of French bread. Then he spread some butter on the bottom slice of bread. After that, he carefully added sweet pickles. On top of that he added cold meat. Next, came some cheese. Then Clark placed the tomatoes and, finally, the lettuce.

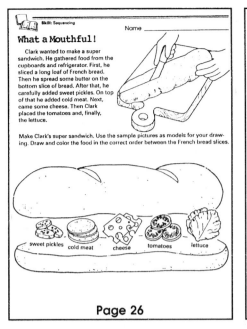

Make Clark's super sandwich. Use the sample pictures as models for your drawing. Draw and color the food in the correct order between the French bread slices.

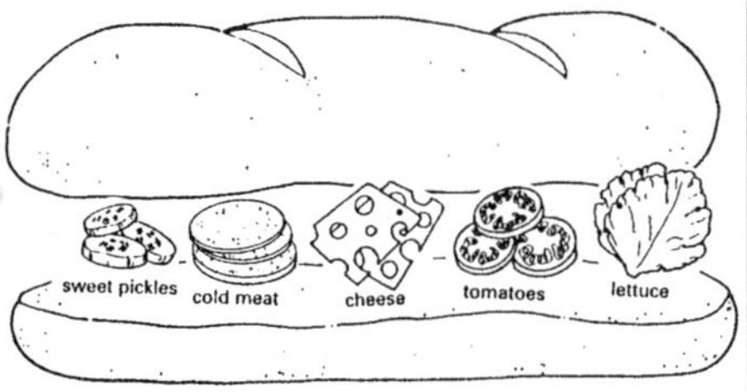

Page 26

Skill: Character Analysis

Name ____________

The Blizzard

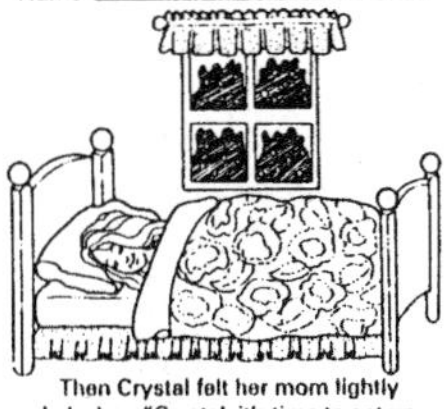

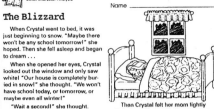

When Crystal went to bed, it was just beginning to snow. "Maybe there won't be any school tomorrow!" she hoped. Then she fell asleep and began to dream . . .

When she opened her eyes, Crystal looked out the window and only saw white! "Our house is completely buried in snow!" she thought. "We won't have school today, or tomorrow, or maybe even all winter!"

"Wait a second!" she thought. "Now I won't be able to see my friends. I can't visit Grandma and Grandpa. Who knows when I will go to the store or the movies, or anywhere again!" Crystal was worried but fell back to sleep.

Then Crystal felt her mom lightly shake her. "Crystal, it's time to get up and go to school."

Crystal raced to the window. There was only an inch of snow on the ground. "I'll be ready in a few minutes," she said as she began to grin.

Use the Word Bank to write how Crystal feels in each sentence.

Word Bank	happy	excited	worried	hopeful

1. Crystal sees the snow begin to fall and thinks that maybe there won't be school tomorrow. She feels hopeful.
2. When she sees the heavy snowfall, Crystal realizes that school will be closed. She feels excited.
3. Then Crystal realizes she won't see friends and grandparents if she can't leave the house. She feels worried.
4. When Crystal gets out of bed she realizes she was dreaming. Crystal feels happy.

Extension: Write how you feel when you discover school will be closed for the day.

Page 27

Skill: Recognizing Details

Name ____________

Grandma's Birthday

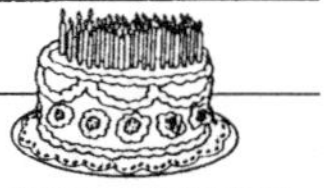

Grandma Tortoise was having another birthday. Her friends decided to throw a party for her and give funny presents because Grandma loved to laugh.

Grandma finally arrived at the party—late as usual! "I had to stop at the Shell Station," she giggled.

Then the hare announced, "I planned a race for your party, but then I remembered that you always win. So, I'll save time and give you the trophy now!"

Grandma got lots of presents, but she had two favorites. The first was a green army helmet. Grandma chuckled when she took it from the box. "It reminds me of my first boyfriend. He had the best-looking shell in town," she remarked.

The other present that Grandma liked was a sweater with tiny yarn people sewn all around the neck. Grandma had lots of turtleneck sweaters, but this was her only "people-neck" sweater.

At last, it was time for the cake and ice cream. There was only one problem. The ice cream had melted by the time Grandma had blown out all of the candles! Everyone agreed that at Grandma's next birthday party they would eat the ice cream first!

Circle the correct detail in each sentence.

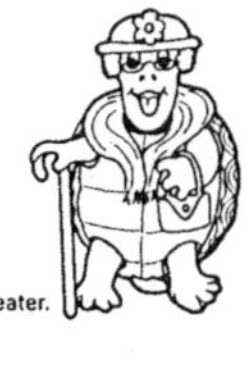

Grandma Tortoise was early / (late) for her birthday party.

The hare thought Grandma (would) / would not win the race.

The army helmet reminded her of an old (boyfriend) / hat.

Little yarn turtles / (people) were sewn on the neck of the sweater.

Circle Yes or No for each sentence.

Grandma liked . . .			
	to be on time.	Yes	(No)
	to laugh.	(Yes)	No
	funny presents.	(Yes)	No
	her sweater.	(Yes)	No

Page 28

Skill: Main Idea

Name ____________

Look Out Below!

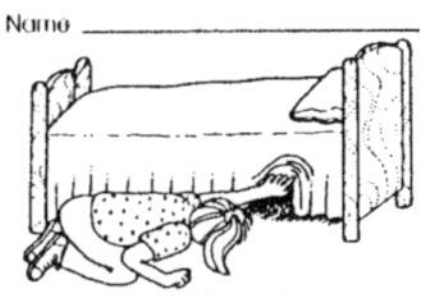

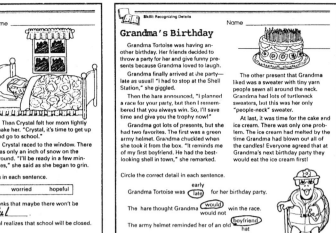

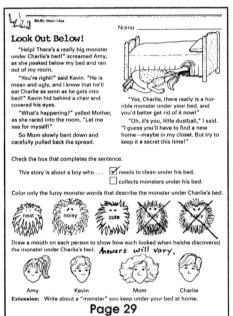

"Help! There's a really big monster under Charlie's bed!" screamed Amy, as she peeked below my bed and ran out of my room.

"You're right!" said Kevin. "He is mean and ugly, and I know that he'll eat Charlie as soon as he gets into bed!" Kevin hid behind a chair and covered his eyes.

"What's happening?" yelled Mother, as she raced into the room. "Let me see for myself!"

So Mom slowly bent down and carefully pulled back the spread.

"Yes, Charlie, there really is a horrible monster under your bed, and you'd better get rid of it now!"

"Oh, it's you, little dustball," I said. "I guess you'll have to find a new home—maybe in my closet. But try to keep it a secret this time!"

Check the box that completes the sentence.

This story is about a boy who . . .
- ☑ needs to clean under his bed.
- ☐ collects monsters under his bed.

Color only the fuzzy monster words that describe the monster under Charlie's bed.

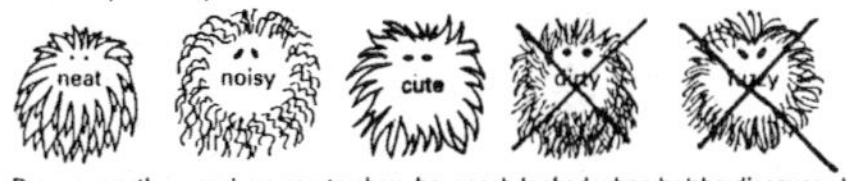

Draw a mouth on each person to show how each looked when he/she discovered the monster under Charlie's bed. Answers will vary.

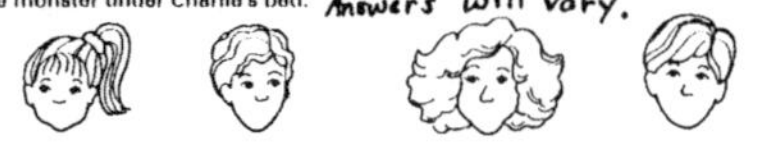

Extension: Write about a "monster" you keep under your bed at home.

Page 29

Skill: Sequencing

Name ____________

Too Much TV

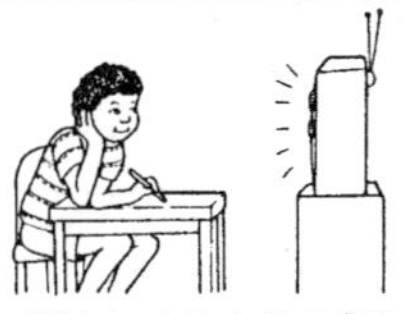

Telly watched TV whenever he could. Every day he turned on the television as soon as he hopped out of the bed. When he came home from school, his right hand was on the remote control as soon as his left hand closed the door. Telly excused himself from dinner to secretly watch more TV. He even sat in front of the set while he did his homework.

One day something very strange happened. Telly's head started becoming square-shaped. Then, he grew a V-shaped antenna on the top of his head! Buttons and numbers appeared on his chest. Telly was turning into a TV!

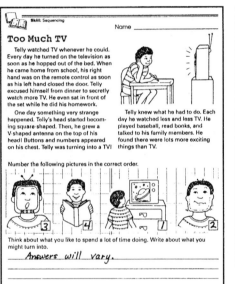

Telly knew what he had to do. Each day he watched less and less TV. He played baseball, read books, and talked to his family members. He found there were lots more exciting things than TV.

Number the following pictures in the correct order.

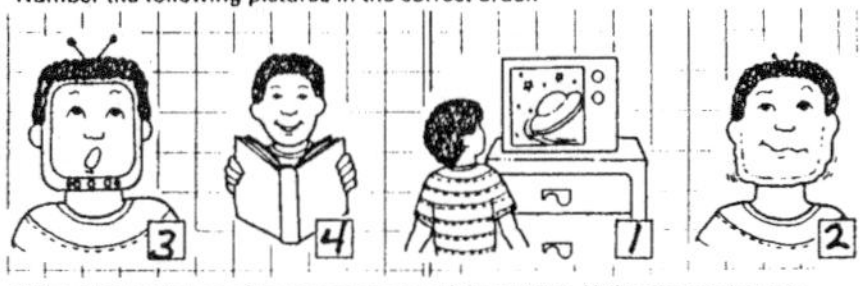

Think about what you like to spend a lot of time doing. Write about what you might turn into.

Answers will vary.

Page 30

Skill: Character Analysis

Name ____________

This Little Piggy . . .

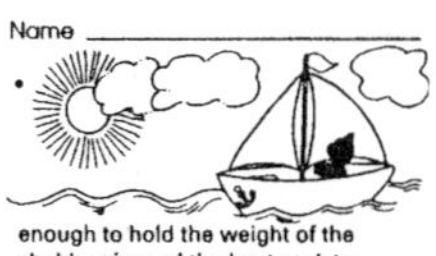

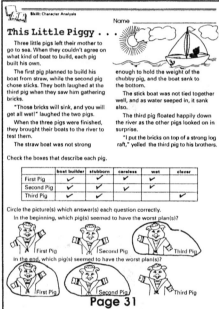

Three little pigs left their mother to go to sea. When they couldn't agree on what kind of boat to build, each pig built his own.

The first pig planned to build his boat from straw, while the second pig chose sticks. They both laughed at the third pig when they saw him gathering bricks.

"Those bricks will sink, and you will get all wet!" laughed the two pigs.

When the three pigs were finished, they brought their boats to the river to test them.

The straw boat was not strong enough to hold the weight of the chubby pig, and the boat sank to the bottom.

The stick boat was not tied together well, and as water seeped in, it sank also.

The third pig floated happily down the river as the other pigs looked on in surprise.

"I put the bricks on top of a strong log raft," yelled the third pig to his brothers.

Check the boxes that describe each pig.

	boat builder	stubborn	careless	wet	clever
First Pig	✓	✓	✓	✓	
Second Pig	✓	✓	✓	✓	
Third Pig	✓	✓			✓

Circle the picture(s) which answer(s) each question correctly.

In the beginning, which pig(s) seemed to have the worst plan(s)?

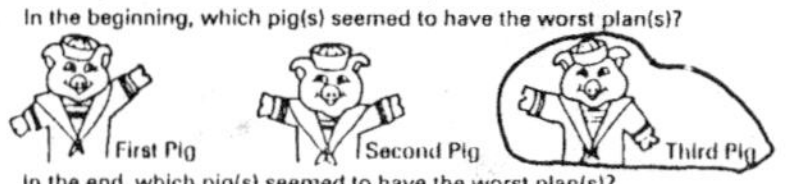

In the end, which pig(s) seemed to have the worst plan(s)?

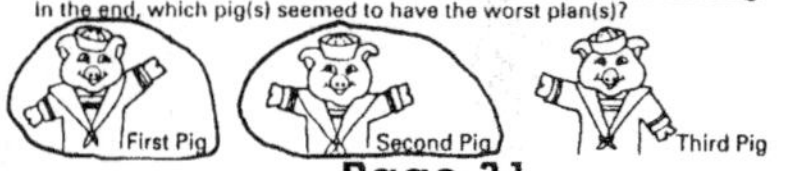

Page 31

Skill: Inference

Name ____________

Home Sweet Home

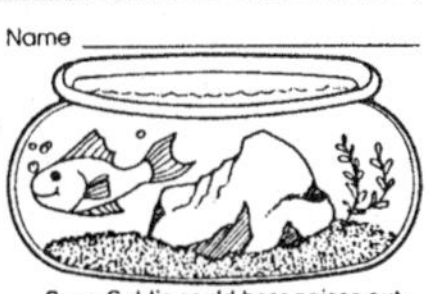

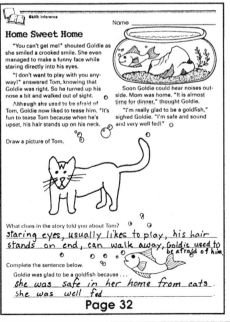

"You can't get me!" shouted Goldie as she smiled a crooked smile. She even managed to make a funny face while staring directly into his eyes.

"I don't want to play with you anyway!" answered Tom, knowing that Goldie was right. So he turned up his nose a bit and walked out of sight.

Although she used to be afraid of Tom, Goldie now liked to tease him. "It's fun to tease Tom because when he's upset, his hair stands up on his neck.

Soon Goldie could hear noises outside. Mom was home. "It is almost time for dinner," thought Goldie.

"I'm really glad to be a goldfish," sighed Goldie. "I'm safe and sound and very well fed!"

Draw a picture of Tom.

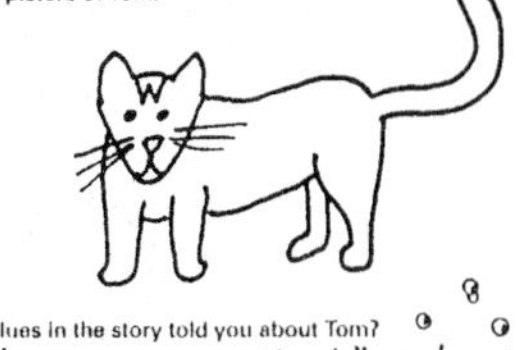

What clues in the story told you about Tom?

staring eyes, usually likes to play, his hair stands on end, can walk away, Goldie used to be afraid of him.

Complete the sentence below.

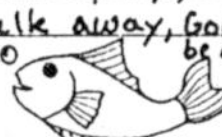

Goldie was glad to be a goldfish because . . .

she was safe in her home from cats. she was well fed.

Page 32

Skill: Similarities and Differences

Name ____________

Grin and Bear It!

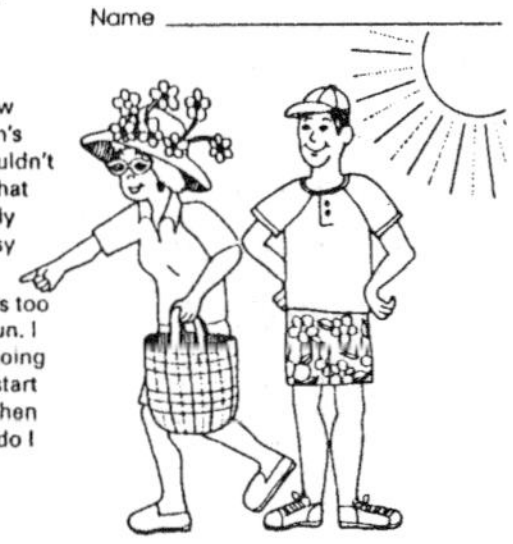

Hey, Winnie! Here comes a new group of people. Look at that man's funny, flowered shorts. I sure wouldn't want to be seen wearing them. That lady has a hat that would probably look better as a flower pot. A daisy could be growing from it.

They all just point and stare. It's too hot to be standing in the direct sun. I wonder how they cool off. I'm going to go swimming. Maybe they'll start throwing treats if I roll over and then sit up. Everyone loves that. Boy, do I have them trained!

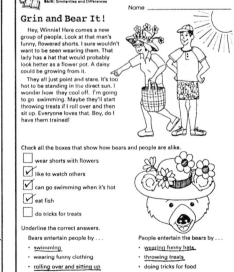

Check all the boxes that show how bears and people are alike.

- ☐ wear shorts with flowers
- ☑ like to watch others
- ☑ can go swimming when it's hot
- ☑ eat fish
- ☐ do tricks for treats

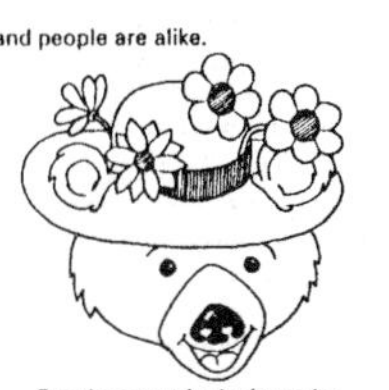

Underline the correct answers.

Bears entertain people by . . .
- swimming (underlined)
- wearing funny clothing
- rolling over and sitting up (underlined)

People entertain the bears by . . .
- wearing funny hats (underlined)
- throwing treats (underlined)
- doing tricks for food

Page 33

Skill: Inference

Name ____________

The Investigation

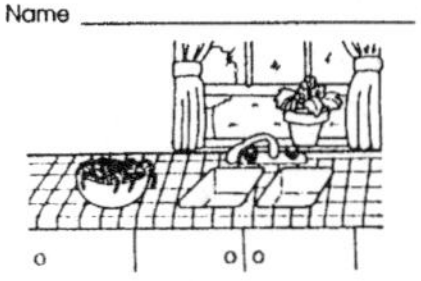

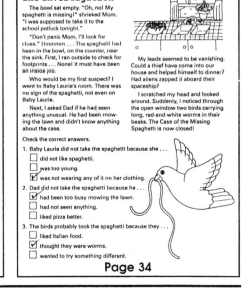

The bowl sat empty. "Oh, no! My spaghetti is missing!" shrieked Mom. "I was supposed to take it to the school potluck tonight."

"Don't panic Mom, I'll look for clues." Hmmmm . . . The spaghetti had been in the bowl, on the counter, near the sink. First, I ran outside to check for footprints . . . None! It must have been an inside job.

Who would be my first suspect? I went to Baby Laurie's room. There was no sign of the spaghetti, not even on Baby Laurie.

Next, I asked Dad if he had seen anything unusual. He had been mowing the lawn and didn't know anything about the case.

My leads seemed to be vanishing. Could a thief have come into our house and helped himself to dinner? Had aliens zapped it aboard their spaceship?

I scratched my head and looked around. Suddenly, I noticed through the open window two birds carrying long, red-and-white worms in their beaks. The Case of the Missing Spaghetti is now closed!

Check the correct answers.

1. Baby Laurie did not take the spaghetti because she . . .
   - ☐ did not like spaghetti.
   - ☐ was too young.
   - ☑ was not wearing any of it on her clothing.
2. Dad did not take the spaghetti because he . . .
   - ☑ had been too busy mowing the lawn.
   - ☐ had not seen anything.
   - ☐ liked pizza better.
3. The birds probably took the spaghetti because they . . .
   - ☐ liked Italian food.
   - ☑ thought they were worms.
   - ☐ wanted to try something different.

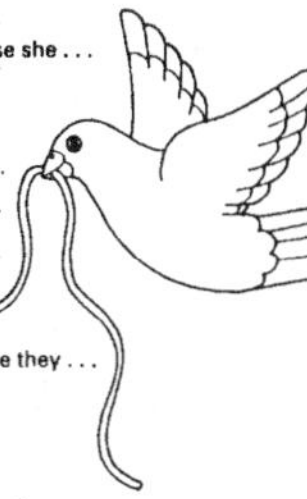

Page 34

The Cure
Name _____

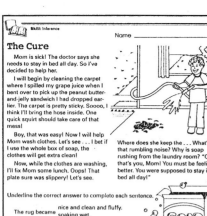

Mom is sick! The doctor says she needs to stay in bed all day. So I've decided to help her.

I will begin by cleaning the carpet where I spilled my grape juice when I bent over to pick up the peanut butter-and-jelly sandwich I had eaten earlier. The carpet is pretty sticky. Soooo, I think I'll bring the hose inside. One quick squirt should take care of that mess!

Boy, that was easy! Now I will help Mom wash clothes. Let's see . . . I bet if I use the whole box of soap, the clothes will get extra clean!

Now, while the clothes are washing, I'll fix Mom some lunch. Oops! That plate sure was slippery! Let's see.

Where does she keep the . . . What's that rumbling noise? Why is soap rushing from the laundry room? "Oh, that's you, Mom! You must be feeling better. You were supposed to stay in bed all day!"

Underline the correct answer to complete each sentence.

The rug became **soaking wet**.

The washing machine **overflowed**.

Mom probably **fixed her own lunch**.

Circle Yes or No for each sentence.

The child tried to make a mess. Yes / **No**

The child wants to help his mom. **Yes** / No

Mom probably told her child to go out and play. **Yes** / No

Extension: Draw a picture of yourself helping your mom when she is sick.

Page 35

A Royal Smile
Name _____

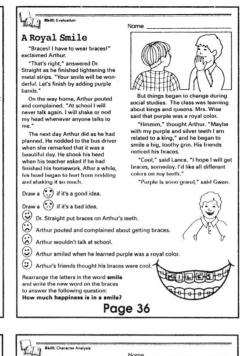

"Braces! I have to wear braces!" exclaimed Arthur.

"That's right," answered Dr. Straight as he finished tightening the metal strips. "Your smile will be wonderful. Let's finish by adding purple bands."

On the way home, Arthur pouted and complained. "At school I will never talk again. I will shake or nod my head whenever anyone talks to me."

The next day Arthur did as he had planned. He nodded to the bus driver when she remarked that it was a beautiful day. He shook his head when his teacher asked if he had finished his homework. After a while, his head began to hurt from nodding and shaking it so much.

But things began to change during social studies. The class was learning about kings and queens. Mrs. Wise said that purple was a royal color.

"Hmmm," thought Arthur. "Maybe with my purple and silver teeth I am related to a king," and he began to smile a big, toothy grin. His friends noticed his braces.

"Cool," said Lance. "I hope I will get braces, someday. I'd like all different colors on my teeth."

"Purple is sooo grand," said Gwen.

Draw a ☺ if it's a good idea.

Draw a ☹ if it's a bad idea.

☹ Dr. Straight put braces on Arthur's teeth.

☹ Arthur pouted and complained about getting braces.

☹ Arthur wouldn't talk at school.

☺ Arthur smiled when he learned purple was a royal color.

☺ Arthur's friends thought his braces were cool.

Rearrange the letters in the word **smile** and write the new word on the braces to answer the following question:
How much happiness is in a smile?

Page 36

That's a Pizza!
Name _____

Papa Luigi is having a bad day. He forgot to order some things that he uses to make his very special pizza.

Pete walked into the restaurant. "I'd like to order your 'Papa Luigi's Pizza Supremo'," he stated.

"I'm sorry, but I do not have all of the toppings," explained Papa Luigi. "However, I will make one large surprise pizza at a special price of $5.00."

"Okay," said Pete.

"Pizza good sport!" thought Luigi.

Use the clues to find what toppings were on the pizza.

1. c h e e s e (rhymes with sneeze)
2. T o m ato (Thomas's nickname)
3. saus a g e (the number of years one has lived)
4. pine a p p l e (a red fruit)
5. o l i v e s (opposite of die)

Now discover what toppings were missing.

1. mush r o o m s (areas in a house)
2. g r e e n peppers ("go" on a stoplight)
3. g r o u n d beef (shape of a circle)
4. p e p p e r oni (opposite of salt)
5. o n i o n s (opposite of off—twice)

Page 37

The Inventor
Name _____

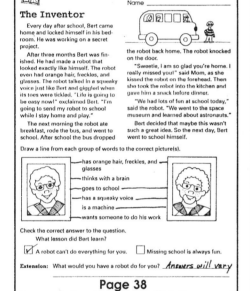

Every day after school, Bert came home and locked himself in his bedroom. He was working on a secret project.

After three months Bert was finished. He had made a robot that looked exactly like himself. The robot even had orange hair, freckles, and glasses. The robot talked in a squeaky voice just like Bert and giggled when its toes were tickled. "Life is going to be easy now!" exclaimed Bert. "I'm going to send my robot to school while I stay home and play."

The next morning the robot ate breakfast, rode the bus, and went to school. After school the bus dropped

the robot back home. The robot knocked on the door.

"Sweetie, I am so glad you're home. I really missed you!" said Mom, as she kissed the robot on the forehead. Then she took the robot into the kitchen and gave him a snack before dinner.

"We had lots of fun at school today," said the robot. "We went to the space museum and learned about astronauts."

Bert decided that maybe this wasn't such a great idea. So the next day, Bert went to school himself.

Draw a line from each group of words to the correct picture(s).

- has orange hair, freckles, and glasses
- thinks with a brain
- goes to school
- has a squeaky voice
- is a machine
- wants someone to do his work

Check the correct answer to the question.

What lesson did Bert learn?

☑ A robot can't do everything for you. ☐ Missing school is always fun.

Extension: What would you have a robot do for you? _Answers will vary_

Page 38

The Kiss
Name _____

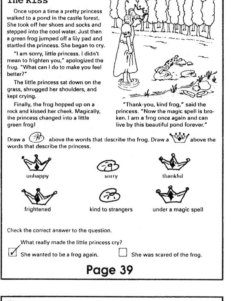

Once upon a time a pretty princess walked to a pond in the castle forest. She took off her shoes and socks and stepped into the cool water. Just then a green frog jumped off a lily pad and startled the princess. She began to cry.

"I am sorry, little princess. I didn't mean to frighten you," apologized the frog. "What can I do to make you feel better?"

The little princess sat down on the grass, shrugged her shoulders, and kept crying.

Finally, the frog hopped up on a rock and kissed her cheek. Magically, the princess changed into a little green frog!

"Thank-you, kind frog," said the princess. "Now the magic spell is broken. I am a frog once again and can live by this beautiful pond forever."

Draw a 🐸 above the words that describe the frog. Draw a 👑 above the words that describe the princess.

👑 unhappy   🐸 sorry   🐸 thankful

👑 frightened   🐸 kind to strangers   👑 under a magic spell

Check the correct answer to the question.

What really made the little princess cry?

☑ She wanted to be a frog again. ☐ She was scared of the frog.

Page 39

My Haunted House
Name _____

I know that our house is haunted, but I still get blamed for everything that goes wrong! I pick up my toys when I'm finished playing, but Dad always seems to be tripping over one of them. I hang my clothes in the closet, but Mom says she finds them all over the floor. Even my big sister accuses me of getting into her things. I would never do that or any of the other things I'm blamed for. Why is that ghost trying to get me in trouble?

Read what it says under each window in the house. Draw a face in the window that states the main idea. Draw a ghost in all of the windows that are supporting details.

Clothes are not hung in closet. | Toys are not put away. | Bedroom is not in neat order.
Uses his sister's things without asking. | | The child is either forgetful or naughty.

Rewrite the main idea sentence from the windows to help the child solve the problem.
The child will remember to be responsible.

Extension: Write two ways the "ghost" in your house gets you in trouble.

1. _Answers will vary_
2. ____

Page 40

Time Machine
Name _____

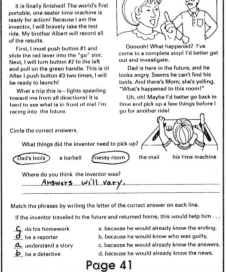

It is finally finished! The world's first portable, one-seater time machine is ready for action! Because I am the inventor, I will bravely take the test ride. My brother Albert will record all of the results.

First, I must push button #1 and slide the red lever into the "go" slot. Next, I will turn button #2 to the left and pull on the green handle. This is it! After I push button #3 two times, I will be ready to launch!

What a trip this is—lights speeding toward me from all directions! It is hard to see what is in front of me! I'm racing into the future.

Ooooooh! What happened? I've come to a complete stop! I'd better get out and investigate.

Dad is here in the future, and he looks angry. Seems he can't find his tools. And there's Mom; she's yelling, "What's happened to this room!"

Uh, oh! Maybe I'd better go back in time and pick up a few things before I go for another ride!

Circle the correct answers.

What things did the inventor need to pick up?

Dad's tools   a barbell   **messy room**   the mail   his time machine

Where do you think the inventor was?
Answers will vary.

Match the phrases by writing the letter of the correct answer on each line.

If the inventor traveled to the future and returned home, this would help him . . .

_c_ do his homework   a. because he would already know the ending.
_d_ be a reporter   b. because he would know who was guilty.
_a_ understand a story   c. because he would already know the answers.
_b_ be a detective   d. because he would already know the news.

Page 41

Mind Game
Name _____

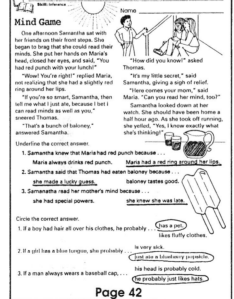

One afternoon Samantha sat with her friends on their front steps. She began to brag that she could read their minds. She put her hands on Maria's head, closed her eyes, and said, "You had red punch with your lunch!"

"Wow! You're right!" replied Maria, not realizing that she had a slightly red ring around her lips.

"If you're so smart, Samantha, then tell me what I just ate, because I bet I can read minds as well as you," sneered Thomas.

"That's a bunch of baloney," answered Samantha.

"How did you know!" asked Thomas.

"It's my little secret," said Samantha, giving a sigh of relief.

"Here comes your mom," said Maria. "Can you read her mind, too?"

Samantha looked down at her watch. She should have been home a half hour ago. As she took off running, she yelled, "Yes, I know exactly what she's thinking!"

Underline the correct answer.

1. Samantha knew that Maria had red punch because . . .
   Maria always drinks red punch. / **Maria had a red ring around her lips.**

2. Samantha said that Thomas had eaten baloney because . . .
   she made a lucky guess. / baloney tastes good.

3. Samantha read her mother's mind because . . .
   she had special powers. / **she knew she was late.**

Circle the correct answer.

1. If a boy had hair all over his clothes, he probably . . . **has a pet.** / likes fluffy clothes.

2. If a girl has a blue tongue, she probably . . . is very sick. / **just ate a blueberry popsicle.**

3. If a man always wears a baseball cap, . . . his head is probably cold. / **he probably just likes hats.**

Page 42

Bath Time Blues
Name _____

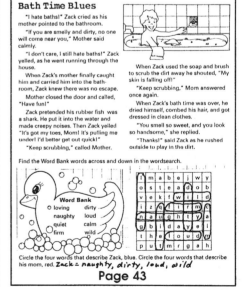

"I hate baths!" Zack cried as his mother pointed to the bathroom.

"If you are smelly and dirty, no one will come near you," Mother said calmly.

"I don't care, I still hate baths!" Zack yelled, as he went running through the house.

When Zack's mother finally caught him and carried him into the bathroom, Zack knew there was no escape.

Mother closed the door and called, "Have fun!"

Zack pretended his rubber fish was a shark. He put it into the water and made creepy noises. Then Zack yelled "It's got my toes, Mom! It's pulling me under! I'd better get out quick!"

"Keep scrubbing," called Mother.

When Zack used the soap and brush to scrub the dirt away he shouted, "My skin is falling off!"

"Keep scrubbing," Mom answered once again.

When Zack's bath time was over, he dried himself, combed his hair, and got dressed in clean clothes.

"You smell so sweet, and you look so handsome," she replied.

"Thanks!" said Zack as he rushed outside to play in the dirt.

Find the Word Bank words across and down in the wordsearch.

Word Bank
○ loving   ○ dirty
○ naughty   ○ loud
○ quiet   ○ calm
○ firm   ○ wild

Circle the four words that describe Zack, blue. Circle the four words that describe his mom, red. _Zack = naughty, dirty, loud, wild_

Page 43
